ABOUT THE ROYAL SHAKESPEARE COMPANY

The Shakespeare Memorial Theatre opened in Stratford-upon-Avon in 1879. Since then the plays of Shakespeare have been performed here, alongside the work of his contemporaries and of modern playwrights. In 1960 the Royal Shakespeare Company was formed, gaining its Royal Charter in 1961.

The founding Artistic Director, Peter Hall, created an ensemble theatre company of young actors and writers. The Company was led by Hall, Peter Brook and Michel Saint-Denis. The founding principles were threefold: the Company would embrace the freedom and power of Shakespeare's work, train and develop young actors and directors and, crucially, experiment in new ways of making theatre. There was a new spirit amongst this post-war generation and they intended to open up Shakespeare's plays as never before.

The impact of Peter Hall's vision cannot be underplayed. In 1955 he premiered Samuel Beckett's *Waiting for Godot* in London, and the result was like opening a window during a storm. The tumult of new ideas emerging across Europe in art, theatre and literature came flooding into British theatre. Hall channelled this new excitement into the setting up of the Company in Stratford. Exciting breakthroughs took place in the rehearsal room and the studio day after day. The RSC became known for exhilarating performances of Shakespeare alongside new masterpieces such as *The ~~~~~~~~~~* and *Old Times* by Harold Pinter ~~~~~~~~~~~~~~~~~~~~ liences.

Peter Hall's rigour on c ~~~~~~~~~~~~~~~~~~~~~~~~ nat is little known is that he ~~~~~~~~~~~~~~~~~~~~~~~~~ g on Beckett, and later on Ha ~~~~~~~~~~~~~~~~~~~~~~~~ e, and likewise he applied ever ~~~~~~~~~~~~~~ ... Shakespeare onto modern texts. This close and exacting relationship between writers from different eras became the fuel which powered the creativity of the RSC.

The search for new forms of writing and directing was led by Peter Brook. He pushed writers to experiment. "Just as Picasso set out to capture a larger slice of the truth by painting a face with several eyes and noses, Shakespeare, knowing that man is living his everyday life and at the same time is living intensely in the invisible world of his thoughts and feelings, developed a method through which we can see at one and the same time the look on a man's face and the vibrations of his brain."

In over fifty years of producing new plays, we have sought out some of the most exciting writers of their generation. These have included: Edward Albee, Howard Barker, Edward Bond, Howard Brenton, Marina Carr, Caryl Churchill, Martin Crimp, David Edgar, Helen Edmundson, James Fenton, Georgia Fitch, David Greig, Ella Hickson, Dennis Kelly, Tarell Alvin McCraney, Martin McDonagh, Frank McGuinness, Rona Munro, Anthony Neilson, Harold Pinter, Phil Porter, Mike Poulton, Mark Ravenhill, Adriano Shaplin, Tom Stoppard, debbie tucker green, Peter Whelan and Roy Williams.

The Company today is led by Gregory Doran, whose appointment represents a long-term commitment to the disciplines and craftsmanship required to put on the plays of Shakespeare. He, along with Executive Director, Catherine Mallyon, and his Deputy Artistic Director, Erica Whyman, take forward a belief in celebrating both Shakespeare's work and the work of his contemporaries, as well as inviting some of the most exciting theatre-makers of today to work with the Company on new plays.

The RSC Ensemble is generously supported by THE GATSBY CHARITABLE FOUNDATION and THE KOVNER FOUNDATION.

The RSC Literary Department is generously supported by THE DRUE HEINZ TRUST.

The 'Roaring Girls' season is generously supported by Miranda Curtis.

The RSC is grateful for the significant support of its principal funder, Arts Council England, without which our work would not be possible. Around 73 per cent of the RSC's income is self-generated from Box Office sales, sponsorship, donations, enterprise and partnerships with other organisations.

Supported using public funding by
ARTS COUNCIL ENGLAND

NEW WORK AT THE RSC

We are a contemporary theatre company built on classical rigour. Through an extensive programme of research and development, we resource writers, directors and actors to explore and develop new ideas for our stages, and as part of this we commission playwrights to engage with the muscularity and ambition of the classics and to set Shakespeare's world in the context of our own. In 2015 we intend to re-open The Other Place in Stratford-upon-Avon, which will be a creative home for new work and experimentation. Leading up to that reopening we will continue to find spaces and opportunities to offer our audiences contemporary voices alongside our classical repertoire.

We invite writers to spend time with us in our rehearsal rooms, with our actors and creative teams. Alongside developing their own plays for all our stages, we invite them to contribute dramaturgically to both our main stage Shakespeare productions and our work for young people. We believe that engaging with living writers and other contemporary theatre makers helps to establish a creative culture within the Company which both inspires new work and creates an ever more urgent sense of enquiry into the classics. Shakespeare was a great innovator and breaker of rules, as well as a bold commentator on the times in which he lived. It is his spirit of 'radical mischief' which informs new work at the RSC.

Erica Whyman, Deputy Artistic Director, heads up this strand of the Company's work alongside Pippa Hill as Literary Manager.

MIDSUMMER MISCHIEF

The plays in this Festival are intended to be a contemporary response to 2014's 'Roaring Girls' season in the Swan Theatre, Stratford-upon-Avon, so we gave our writers — Alice Birch, E. V. Crowe, Timberlake Wertenbaker and Abi Zakarian an initial provocation: 'Well-behaved women seldom make history' (Laurel Thatcher Ulrich). These daring and radical plays are presented as two short programmes, each playing in repertoire with a shared cast. We hope you're feeling mischievous…

The *Midsummer Mischief* Festival was first presented by the Royal Shakespeare Company in The Other Place at the Courtyard Theatre, Stratford-upon-Avon, on 14 June 2014. The Festival transferred to the Jerwood Theatre Upstairs, Royal Court on 15 July 2014. The cast was as follows:

PROGRAMME A

The Ant and the Cicada by Timberlake Wertenbaker

Student	**Robert Boulter**
Alex	**John Bowe**
Student	**Scarlett Brookes**
Selina	**Ruth Gemmell**
Zoe	**Julie Legrand**
Irina	**Mimi Ndiweni**

Revolt. She said. Revolt again. by Alice Birch

Company	**Robert Boulter**
Company	**Scarlett Brookes**
Company	**Ruth Gemmell**
Company	**Mimi Ndiweni**

PROGRAMME B

I Can Hear You by E.V. Crowe

Tommy	**Robert Boulter**
David	**John Bowe**
Ellie	**Scarlett Brookes**
Ruth	**Ruth Gemmell**
Sandra	**Mimi Ndiweni**

This is Not an Exit by Abi Zakarian

Gulch	**Scarlett Brookes**
Nora	**Ruth Gemmell**
Blanche	**Julie Legrand**
Ripley	**Mimi Ndiweni**

PROGRAMME A

Directed by	**Erica Whyman**
Designed by	**Madeleine Girling**
Lighting Designed by	**Claire Gerrens**
Sound by	**Jonathan Ruddick**
Dramaturgs	**Sarah Dickenson** (*Revolt. She said. Revolt again.*) **Pippa Hill** (*The Ant and the Cicada*)
Assistant Director	**Joseph Wilde**

PROGRAMME B

Directed by	**Jo McInnes**
Designed by	**Max Dorey**
Lighting Designed by	**Robin Griggs**
Composer (*This is Not an Exit*)	**Johanna Groot Bluemink**
Sound by	**Jon Lawrence**
Dramaturgs	**Sarah Dickenson** (*This is Not an Exit*) **Pippa Hill** (*I Can Hear You*)
Assistant Director	**Anthony Ekundayo Lennon**

MIDSUMMER MISCHIEF FESTIVAL

Producer	**Claire Birch**
Literary Manager	**Pippa Hill**
Literary Projects Coordinator	**Réjane Collard**
Literary Assistant	**Collette McCarthy**
Company Text and Voice Work	**Nia Lynn**
Casting by	**Hannah Miller** CDG **Annelie Powell**
Production Manager	**David Tanqueray**
Costume Supervisor	**Gayle Woodsend**
Company Manager	**Julia Wade**
Assistant Stage Managers	**Rachel Harris** **Martha Mamo**
Overview Design	**Tom Piper**
Studio Design and Build	**Tom Piper, Peter Bailey, Julian Cree, David Tanqueray**
Technicians	**Delfina Angiolini, Jon Lawrence, Tim Owen, Sarah Ware**

This edition of the plays went to print before the end of rehearsals and so may differ slightly from the plays as performed.

LOVE THE RSC?

Support us and make a difference

The RSC is a registered charity. We perform all year round in our Stratford-upon-Avon home, as well as having regular seasons in London, and touring extensively within the UK and overseas for international residencies.

By supporting us through RSC Membership or joining the Supporters' Ensemble you will help to fund our work both on and off the stage.

Choose a level that suits you from £18 through to £10,000 per year and enjoy a closer connection with the RSC, whilst at the same time enabling us to continue to make the theatre that you love.

For more information visit **www.rsc.org.uk/supportus** or call the RSC Membership Office on 01789 403440.

CAST

ROBERT BOULTER
RSC DEBUT SEASON: *The Ant and the Cicada, Revolt. She said. Revolt again., I Can Hear You.*
THEATRE INCLUDES: *The Odyssey, Burn/Chatroom/Citizenship, Karamazoo, An Island Far From Here* (National Theatre); *How to Curse* (Bush); *Mercury Fur* (Paines Plough); *Herons* (Royal Court); *A Midsummer Night's Dream* (Jagged Fence); *The Merchant of Venice* (Derby Live).
TELEVISION INCLUDES: *Evidence, Father Brown, Casualty, Survivors, Waking the Dead, The Long Firm, Judge John Deed, Doctors, The Bill.*
FILM INCLUDES: *Some Things Mean Something, Mercenaries, Donkey Punch, Daylight Robbery.*

JOHN BOWE
RSC INCLUDES: *The Wizard of Oz, Cyrano de Bergerac* (LA Olympic Arts Festival/Broadway/ Washington); *The Taming of the Shrew, The Body, Arden of Faversham, Thirteenth Night, As You Like It, Richard II, Richard III, Hamlet, The White Guard, Captain Swing, Antony and Cleopatra, The Merchant of Venice,* Edward Bond's *Lear* (Stratford/European tour).
THIS SEASON: *The Ant and the Cicada, I Can Hear You.*
THEATRE INCLUDES: Billy in *Daytona* (Park Theatre); Judge Turpin in *Sweeney Todd* (Chichester Festival Theatre); Bob in *Priscilla Queen of the Desert* (Palace); *Terms of Endearment* (tour); *The Lady from the Sea, Heartbreak House* (Almeida); *The Marriage of Figaro, The Price* (Watford Palace); *Observe the Sons of Ulster Marching Toward the Somme* (Hampstead); *Othello* (New Shakespeare Company, Regent's Park); *Saint Joan* (Old Vic); *Henry V, Pilgrim, The Royal Hunt of the Sun* (Prospect/UK and world tour).
TELEVISION INCLUDES: *Murder on the Home Front, DCI Banks, New Tricks, The Hour, Silent Witness, Ashes to Ashes, The Royal, Midsomer Murders, The Bill, Einstein and Eddington, Cranford, Casualty, Dalziel and Pascoe, Heartbeat, Secret Smile, Spine Chillers – The Majister, The Stepfather, Murder in Mind, Tipping the Velvet, Coronation Street, Mrs Bradley, Cleopatra, Split Second, Verdict, Imogen's Face, Bright Hair, Bodyguards, The Prince and the Pauper, Poldark, Soldier Soldier, Class Act, Wall of Silence, Lovejoy, Inspector Alleyn, The New Statesman, Body and Soul, Trainer, Stalin, Boon, Families, Prime Suspect, Capital City, Testimony of a Child, Precious Bane, The One Game, After the War, Gran Jones, Hard Cases, Cats Eyes, Clem, Cyrano de Bergerac, Remington Steel, Warship.*
FILM INCLUDES: *Ruby's Skin, Gozo, Snappers, County Kilburn, Resurrection, The Living Daylights.*
RADIO INCLUDES: *With Great Pleasure, Elephants to Catch Eels.*

SCARLETT BROOKES
RSC DEBUT SEASON: *The Ant and the Cicada, Revolt. She said. Revolt again., I Can Hear You, This is Not an Exit.*
TRAINED: RADA.
THEATRE INCLUDES: *To Kill a Mockingbird* (Royal Exchange); *Ignorance* (Hampstead); *Love and Information* (Royal Court); *Our Big Land* (Romany Theatre Co.).
TELEVISION INCLUDES: *Blackout, Misfits, Doctors.*
RADIO: *A Charles Paris Mystery, Dracula, Blink, Rock Me Amadeus, IZ, Juno and the Paycock.*

RUTH GEMMELL
RSC INCLUDES: *Macbeth, King Lear, Midwinter.*
THIS SEASON: *The Ant and the Cicada, Revolt. She said. Revolt again., I Can Hear You, This is Not an Exit.*
THEATRE INCLUDES: *Betrayal* (Sheffield Crucible); *Sixty Six Books* (Bush/Westminster Abbey); *Death and the Maiden, Les Liaisons Dangereuses* (Salisbury Playhouse); *Riflemind* (Trafalgar Studios); *Helter Skelter/ Land of the Dead* (Bush); *Coram Boy* (National Theatre); *Trip's Cinch* (Southwark Playhouse); *Kick for Touch* (Sheffield Crucible); *Ancient Lights, Nabokov's Gloves* (Hampstead); *The Weir* (Royal Court); *Turn of the Screw* (Hornchurch Queen's); *Othello* (The Railway Tavern); *Measure for Measure* (Chester Gateway); *Uncle Vanya* (Edinburgh Lyceum); *An Ideal Husband* (Edinburgh Lyceum); *The Winter's Tale* (Salisbury Playhouse); *The Second Mrs Tanqueray* (Salisbury Playhouse); *The Importance of Being Earnest* (Edinburgh Lyceum); *'Tis Pity She's a Whore* (Lancaster Playhouse); *The Country Wife* (Lancaster Playhouse); *A Tale of Two Cities* (Glasgow Citizens).
TELEVISION INCLUDES: *Casualty, Silent Witness, Inspector George Gently, Coming Up – Big Girl, Holby City, Utopia, Father Brown, Dancing on the Edge, Inside Men, The Fades, Moving On, Law & Order, Lewis, The Bill, Waking the Dead, EastEnders, Primeval, Trial & Retribution, Poirot, Summerhill Project, Five Days, Frost, Are You Jim's Wife?, Midsomer Murders, Tracey Beaker, Spooks, Murder in Mind, Inspector Lynley Mysteries, Dalziel & Pascoe, Blue Dove, Miller Shorts, Four Feathers, The Alchemists, Macbeth, The Perfect Blue, Peak Practice, Kavanagh QC, Band of Gold, Who Needs a Heart.*
FILM INCLUDES: *Offender, Storage 24, F, Good, January 2nd, Fever Pitch.*

JULIE LEGRAND
RSC INCLUDES: *Romeo and Juliet, Beauty and the Beast, Temptation, Cymbeline, The Revenger's Tragedy, Oedipus.*
THIS SEASON: *The Ant and the Cicada, This is Not an Exit.*
THEATRE INCLUDES: *Remembrance of Things Past, The Forest, The Cherry Orchard, The Critic, The Duchess of Malfi, Way Upstream, The Trojan War Will Not Take Place, Don Quixote* (National Theatre); *To Kill a Mockingbird, The Importance of Being Earnest* (Regent's Park Open Air Theatre); *Wicked* (Apollo Victoria); *The Wizard of Oz* (Royal Festival Hall); *Fiddler on the Roof* (Sheffield Crucible/Savoy); *See How They Run* (Duchess/UK tour); *Arcadia* (Haymarket); *The House of Bernarda Alba* (Lyric Hammersmith/Gielgud); *Vincent River, Apocalyptica, Lion in the Streets* (Hampstead); *Madame de Sade* (Almeida); *Marya* (Old Vic); *The Memory of Water* (Richmond/UK tour); *Susanna Andler* (Chichester/UK tour); *Masterclass* (UK tour); *All's Well That Ends Well* (Manchester Royal Exchange); *Hamlet* (Bristol Old Vic); *Great Expectations* (Gate, Dublin); *The Second Mrs Tanqueray, Chinchilla* (Glasgow Citizens); *The White Devil, The Way of the World, The Seagull* (Glasgow Citizens season at Greenwich Theatre); *The Green Man* (Plymouth Theatre Royal/Bush).

TELEVISION INCLUDES: *Edge of Heaven, Holby City, Doctor Who, Doctors, Casualty, Night and Day, Fields of Gold, Footballers' Wives, North Square, Bad Girls, Starting Out, Kavanagh QC, The Bill, Good Friday 1663, Moving Story, Inspector Morse, Anglo Saxon Attitudes, Sandra and Elaine.*
FILM INCLUDES: *One for the Road, Prick Up Your Ears, Water.*

MIMI NDIWENI
RSC: First Encounters: *The Taming of the Shrew.*
THIS SEASON: *The Ant and the Cicada, Revolt. She said. Revolt again., I Can Hear You, This is Not an Exit.*
THEATRE INCLUDES: *Sky Hawk* (Theatre Clwyd); *Pericles* (rehearsed reading).
THEATRE WHILST TRAINING: *Hamlet, Incomplete and Random Acts of Kindness, A Month in the Country, Beast and Beauties, Bob Cratchit's Wild Christmas Binge.*
FILM INCLUDES: *Jack Ryan: Shadow Recruit, Cinderella, Telling Tales.*
RADIO INCLUDES: *Bernice Summerfield, Cigarettes and Chocolate.*

CREATIVE TEAM

ALICE BIRCH
PLAYWRIGHT
RSC DEBUT SEASON: *Revolt. She said. Revolt again.*

Alice is the winner of the George Devine award, the Arts Foundation award for Playwriting 2014 and is one of the BBC Writersroom 10 for 2014. Writing includes *Little on the Inside* (Almeida/Clean Break); *So Much Once* (24 Hour Celebrity Gala, Old Vic); *Open Court Soap Opera* (Royal Court); *Salt* (Comedie de Valence); *Flying the Nest* (BBC Radio 4), *Many Moons* (Theatre503. Shortlisted for the Susan Smith Blackburn award and published by Oberon Books). She is currently under commission to Clean Break, Pentabus and the Young Vic.

E.V. CROWE
PLAYWRIGHT
RSC DEBUT SEASON:
I Can Hear You.

E.V. Crowe's most recent play, *Virgin*, played at Watford Palace in 2013. *Hero* played at the Royal Court at the end of 2012 in a production directed by Jeremy Herrin, with the support of the NT Studio and Schauspiel in Frankfurt. She made her Royal Court debut in 2010 with *Kin* (also directed by Jeremy Herrin) and was shortlisted for the Most Promising Playwright at the *Evening Standard* Theatre Awards. Credits elsewhere include: *Liar, Liar* produced by Unicorn Theatre; *Young Pretender*, produced by nabokov; *Doris Day* for Clean Break/Soho. A graduate of the Royal Court Young Writers' 'Super Group', she is currently under commission to the Royal Court, the National Theatre and Unicorn Theatre. Crowe is also part of the writing team for a new eight-part series called *Glue* (E4/Eleven Films).

SARAH DICKENSON
DRAMATURG
RSC DEBUT SEASON: *Revolt. She said. Revolt again.*, *This is Not an Exit*.

Sarah is a freelance dramaturg and project manager. She is currently Associate Dramaturg for the RSC, Production Dramaturg for Shakespeare's Globe and a visiting tutor at LAMDA and Goldsmiths. She was formerly Senior Reader at Soho Theatre, Literary Manager for Theatre503, New Writing Associate at the Red Room and founding coordinator of the South West New Writing Network. She has worked on performance projects and artistic development nationally and internationally for a wide range of organisations and theatre makers including writernet, National Theatre, Hampstead Theatre, Kaleider, The Wrong Crowd, Bristol Old Vic, Theatre Bristol, Old Vic New Voices, Liverpool Everyman, Champloo, Ustinov Bath, Plymouth Theatre Royal, Tamasha, Apples and Snakes, Almeida, Hall for Cornwall, The Fence and Churchill Theatre Bromley.

MAX DOREY
DESIGNER
RSC: Max is currently one of two Assistant Designers at the RSC.
THIS SEASON: *I Can Hear You, This is Not an Exit*.
TRAINED: Max trained in Theatre Design at Bristol Old Vic Theatre School and has a BA in English Literature and Theatre Studies from Leeds University. In 2013 he was a finalist for the Linbury Prize for Stage Design, held biannually by the National Theatre, during which he worked with the National Theatre of Scotland.
THEATRE INCLUDES: *Black Jesus*

(Finborough); *The School for Scandal* (Waterloo East); *The Duke in the Darkness, Marguerite* (Tabard Theatre. Both nominated for Off West End awards for Best Set Design); *Oedipus* (Blue Elephant); *Disco Pigs* (Tristan Bates); *The Good Soul of Szechuan* (Bristol Old Vic Studio); *Macbeth* (Redgrave Theatre); *Phaedra's Love, Bad House* (NSDF); *Black Comedy, Playhouse Creatures* (Stage@Leeds). Max has also made puppets for Travelling Light's *Peter Pan* (Bristol Old Vic); *Cinderella* (St James Theatre); *Pinocchio* (Bristol Tobacco Factory); Birmingham Rep Young Company's *20,000 Leagues Under the Sea*; Ravenrock Theatre's *Phaedra's Love* and *The View From Down Here*, which he wrote and directed (Carriageworks).

ANTHONY EKUNDAYO LENNON
ASSISTANT DIRECTOR
RSC DEBUT SEASON: *I Can Hear You, This is Not an Exit*.
THEATRE INCLUDES: As Assistant Director: *Moon on a Rainbow Shawl* (UK tour. Talawa Theatre in association with the National Theatre); *The Epic Adventures of Nhamo and his Sexy Wife Chipo* (Tricycle); *The Ship* (Royal Court); *Crawling in the Dark* (Almeida); *Ragamuffin* (Creative Origins/UK Arts International); *The African Company Presents Richard III* (Collective Artists). As Director: *Enter* (Embassy/Talawa); *A Short Lime* and a black play readings event (National Theatre); *Rise* (Talawa Firsts season); *Winsome's Daughter* (Flipping the Script season/Young Vic); *Embryonica* (Birmingham Arts Festival). As Staff Director: *Moon on a Rainbow Shawl* (National Theatre). As Assistant/Resident Director for Debbie Allen he worked with the all-black cast of *Cat*

on a Hot Tin Roof featuring James Earl Jones, Phylicia Rashad, Sanaa Lathan and Adrian Lester (Novello).

CLAIRE GERRENS
LIGHTING DESIGNER
RSC: Claire joined the RSC Lighting department in 2010.
THIS SEASON: *The Ant and the Cicada, Revolt. She said. Revolt again*.
TRAINED: Technical Theatre Arts course, RADA.
THEATRE INCLUDES: In Claire's four years at Stratford she has worked on a number of productions across the Courtyard, RST, Swan and Roundhouse but her highlights so far include: Lighting Programmer on *The Tempest* with Little Angel Theatre Company (Stratford); Lighting Programmer on *Julius Caesar* (Stratford/UK and international tour); Lighting Programmer and re-lighting on *The Rape of Lucrece* (Stratford/UK, Ireland and international tour); Lighting Programmer on *Cardenio* (Stratford); Lighting Programmer on *Wendy & Peter Pan* (Stratford, Christmas 2013).

MADELEINE GIRLING
DESIGNER
RSC: Since April 2013 Madeleine has been working for the Royal Shakespeare Company in a one-year position as Design Assistant.
THIS SEASON: *The Ant and the Cicada, Revolt. She said. Revolt again.*
TRAINED: Madeleine trained in Theatre Design at the Royal Welsh College of Music and Drama, graduating with a First Class Honours, and receiving the Lord Williams Memorial Prize for Design in 2012. She was awarded as a winner in the Linbury Prize for Stage Design 2013 and will be going on to realise

her winning design for Nottingham Playhouse later this year.

THEATRE INCLUDES: *Gardening for the Unfulfilled and Alienated* (Undeb Theatre); *Tender Napalm*, *How to Curse* (BOVTS Director's Showcase); *A Welshman's Guide to Breaking Up* (Boyo Productions); *Hey Diddle Diddle* (Bristol Old Vic); *The Cagebirds* (LAMDA Director's Showcase); *The Life After — Prelude* (BOV Young Company); *Blood Wedding* (RWCMD Burton Company); *The Ducks* (SEArED Productions).

JOHANNA GROOT BLUEMINK
COMPOSER
RSC: *This is Not an Exit.*
Originally from Virginia, Johanna's musical background is rooted both in classical music and folk music of the American South, particularly blues and religious music. Before commencing her doctoral studies at the Guildhall School with Richard Baker and Julian Philips, she received her BMus and MMus from Conservatorium van Amsterdam, studying with Willem Jeths and Richard Ayres. She has received commissions from Ralph van Raat (piano), the Norfolk Chamber Consort (USA), Izhar Elias (guitar) and David Kweksilber (big band), amongst others. As a student, she has collaborated and written works for the Rosa Ensemble and ASKO/Schoenberg Ensemble. This spring, she composed and directed the music for Guildhall's production of *Hamlet* (directed by Jo McInnes) and premiered a piece for voice, horns and flugelhorn at Wigmore Hall.

JON LAWRENCE
SOUND DESIGNER
RSC: Jon joined the RSC in 2011.
THIS SEASON: *I Can Hear You, This is Not an Exit.*
THEATRE INCLUDES: At his time at the RSC, Jon has operated many shows, including taking *Julius Caesar* on a regional and international tour. He's also worked on *Written on the Heart*, *A Mad World My Masters* and *The Roaring Girl* in the Swan Theatre, and *The Merry Wives of Windsor*, *Hamlet* and *As You Like It* in the Royal Shakespeare Theatre.

JO MCINNES
DIRECTOR
RSC DEBUT SEASON: *I Can Hear You, This is Not an Exit.*
Recent directing work includes *Running On Empty* (Probe/Soho Theatre/UK tour); *Vera, Vera, Vera, Red Bud* (Royal Court); *Marine Parade* (Animalink/Brighton Festival); *Christmas* (Brighton/Bush, London). In 2006 Jo held the position of Artistic Director of New Writing South and she has directed workshops and rehearsed readings of new work for, amongst others, the Royal Court, the Old Vic and Hampstead Theatre. Jo is currently Co-Artistic director of Mob Culture, a new company established to support and develop new artists.

TOM PIPER
OVERVIEW DESIGNER
RSC: *Antony and Cleopatra, Boris Godunov, Much Ado About Nothing, Macbeth, The City Madam, As You Like It, The Grain Store, The Drunks, Antony and Cleopatra, The Histories Cycle, The Broken Heart, Spring Awakening, A Patriot for Me, Much Ado About Nothing, The Spanish Tragedy, Bartholomew Fair,*

Measure for Measure, *Troilus and Cressida*, *A Month in the Country*, *A Midsummer Night's Dream*, *Romeo and Juliet*, *Henry VI*, *Richard III*, *The Tempest*, *King Lear*, *Twelfth Night*, *Hamlet*, *Fit and Proper People* (Soho/RSC).

THEATRE DESIGNS INCLUDE: *The Libertine* (Glasgow Citzens); *Bakersfield Mist* (Duchess); *The Big Meal* (Bath Theatre Royal); *The Birthday Party*, *Blinded by the Sun*, *Oh! What a Lovely War* (National Theatre); *Miss Julie* (Haymarket); *Frame 312*, *A Lie of the Mind*, *Three Days of Rain*, *Helpless* (Donmar Warehouse); *Pants*, *Mince*, *The Duchess of Malfi*, *Twelfth Night*, *Happy Days* (Dundee Rep); *Denial*, *Les Liaisons Dangereuses*, *Ghosts* (Bristol Old Vic); *The Danny Crowe Show* (Bush); *The Frogs*, *The Cherry Orchard* (Nottingham Playhouse); *Stiff!*, *The Master Builder* (Edinburgh Lyceum); *The Crucible*, *Six Characters in Search of an Author*, *The Reluctant Tyrant*, *Plough and the Stars* (Abbey, Dublin); *Vera, Vera, Vera*, *Goodbye to All That* (Royal Court); *Zorro* (Garrick/Paris/Moscow/Tokyo/Holland); *Spyski!* (Lyric Hammersmith); *Dealer's Choice* (Menier Chocolate Factory/Trafalgar Studios); *Fall* (Traverse); *Richard III*, *As You Like It*, *The Tempest* (Bridge Project, Old Vic/BAM); *King Lear* (Glasgow Citizens); *Red Velvet*, *Bracken Moor* (Tricycle); *Pride and Prejudice*, *The Winter's Tale* (Regent's Park Open Air Theatre).

JONATHAN RUDDICK
SOUND DESIGNER
RSC: *Julius Caesar* (Stratford/UK tour/Russia), *Song of Songs*, *Written on the Heart*, *Romeo and Juliet* (re-design), *Morte d'Arthur*. Jonathan currently works in the RSC Sound department.

THIS SEASON: *The Ant and the Cicada*, *Revolt. She said. Revolt again*.

THEATRE INCLUDES: From 1999 to 2006 Jonathan worked for the Baxter Theatre Company in the lighting and sound departments, for which work includes: *The Suip!*, *Glass Roots*, *Vatmaar*, *World in a Guitar*, *Madiba Magic*, *Hamlet*, *Amadeus*, *The Travellers* (Fortune Cookie Company, Adelaide).

TELEVISION INCLUDES: Floor Manager for South African Broadcast Corporation (2003-04), Woman of the Year live event.

TIMBERLAKE WERTENBAKER
PLAYWRIGHT
RSC: *The Love of the Nightingale*, *The Thebans*, *Mephisto* (translation).
THIS SEASON: *The Ant and the Cicada*.

Timberlake grew up in the Basque country near Saint-Jean-de-Luz. She has been Arts Council writer in residence with Shared Experience and at the Royal Court. She was the Royden B Davis visiting professor of drama at Georgetown University, Washington DC, 2005-2006, the Leverhulme Artist in Residence at the Freud Museum in 2011 and is currently Chair in Playwriting at the University of East Anglia. She is the recipient of numerous awards including an Olivier award and the 1990 New York Drama Critics award for Our Country's Good, the Writers' Guild and Susan Smith Blackburn awards for Three Birds Alighting on a Field and the Eileen Anderson Central TV Drama award for *The Love of the Nightingale*.

PRODUCTIONS INCLUDE: *Our Ajax* (Southwark Playhouse); *The Line*

(Arcola); *Galileo's Daughter* (Bath Theatre Royal); *Credible Witness*, *The Break of the Day*, *Three Birds Alighting on a Field*, *Our Country's Good*, *The Grace of Mary Traverse*, *Abel's Sister* (Royal Court); *Ash Girl* (Birmingham Rep); *After Darwin* (Hampstead Theatre).

TRANSLATIONS INCLUDE: *Britannicus* (Wilton's Music Hall); *Phèdre* (Stratford Shakespeare Festival, Ontario); *Antigone* (Southwark Playhouse); *Elektra*, *Hecuba* (ACT, The Getty); *Wild Orchids* (Chichester Festival Theatre); *Filumena* (Peter Hall Company at the Piccadilly); *Jenufa* (Arcola).

TELEVISION/FILM INCLUDES: *The Children* (starring Kim Novak and Ben Kingsley); *Do Not Disturb* (starring Frances Barber, Peter Capaldi).

OPERA: *The Love of the Nightingale* (Sydney Opera House).

RADIO DRAMATISATION INCLUDES: AS Byatt's *Possession* (BBC Radio Woman's Hour); *War & Peace* (BBC).

JOSEPH WILDE
ASSISTANT DIRECTOR
RSC DEBUT SEASON: *The Ant and the Cicada, Revolt. She said. Revolt again.*

TRAINED: Joseph studied at the University of East Anglia, trained as an actor at the Oxford School of Drama, as a writer at the Chichester Festival Theatre and Royal Court, and as a director at the Young Vic on their Springboard scheme.

THEATRE INCLUDES: As Director: *Kaleidoscope* (Ovalhouse Young Company); *Jeremy Kyle Nativity Special* (Old Red Lion); *Our Brave New Future* (Sell A Door/Rosemary Branch). As Dramaturg: *Osama Bin Laden: The One Man Show* (Knaive/Edinburgh Fringe/Teatret Katapult);

Here Lies Leonard Langley (Lacuna).

WRITING INCLUDES: *Cuddles* (Ovalhouse); *Wildsong* (Radio 4); *The Loving Ballad of Captain Bateman* (Radio 4. Winner of the Imison award 2014). Joseph was an Escalator Playwright for Hightide Festival Theatre 2013 and writes for BBC Drama.

ERICA WHYMAN
DIRECTOR
RSC: Erica joined the RSC as Deputy Artistic Director in January 2013. She takes a lead on the permanent redevelopment of The Other Place and the programming of new work at the RSC. She will be directing *The Christmas Truce*, **a new play by Phil Porter, for the company's 2014 winter season.**

THIS SEASON: *The Ant and the Cicada, Revolt. She said. Revolt again.*

THEATRE: Erica was Chief Executive of Northern Stage in Newcastle Upon Tyne from 2005 to 2012. Under her stewardship Northern Stage became known for ambitious international partnerships, the development of experimental new work especially by young theatre makers and for bold interpretations of modern classics. Erica was Artistic Director of Southwark Playhouse (1998-2000) and then Artistic Director of the Gate Theatre, Notting Hill (2000-2004). Her directing credits include: for Northern Stage: *Son of Man, Ruby Moon, Our Friends in the North, A Christmas Carol, A Doll's House, Look Back in Anger, Hansel and Gretel, Oh What a Lovely War* (nominated for two TMA awards), *The Wind in the Willows, Who's Afraid of Virginia Woolf* (nominated for Best Director, TMA awards), *The Glass Slipper* and the UK premiere of *Oh, the Humanity*

(Edinburgh/Soho Theatre). Other work includes: *The Birthday Party* (Sheffield Crucible); *The Shadow of a Boy* (National Theatre); *The Flu Season, Marieluise, Witness, Les Justes* (Gate); *The Winter's Tale, The Glass Slipper* (Southwark Playhouse). In 2012 she won the TMA award for Theatre Manager of the Year and was awarded an OBE in 2013 for services to British Theatre.

ABI ZAKARIAN
PLAYWRIGHT
RSC DEBUT SEASON: *This is Not an Exit*.
Abi is the author of six full-length plays: *Lulu7*, produced by So & So Arts at the Tristan Bates Theatre; *Build Lilli*, workshop and rehearsed reading by So & So Arts; *Swifter, Higher, Stronger*, produced by Roundpeg Theatre at the Roundhouse; *Little Furies*, which was commissioned by and received a rehearsed reading at Soho Theatre; *A Thousand Yards*, which was produced by Feast Theatre at Southwark Playhouse; and *Tomorrow*, which received a rehearsed reading produced by the Caird Company. She has also written a short play, *Rip Her to Shreds*, for Undeb Theatre.
Previously a writer on attachment at Soho Theatre and a current member of the RSC's writers group, she is one of the writers involved in the playwright-in-residence Schoolwrights scheme in East London schools.
Abi is currently working on a television comedy series, *I Am Become Jeff*.

Midsummer Mischief is an experiment. It is our attempt to recapture the original spirit of The Other Place by commissioning daring new plays and producing them in six short weeks for a pop-up theatre in Stratford-upon-Avon. It has required courage and creativity in equal measure from everyone involved to make it a reality, but perhaps most especially from our writers, our dramaturgs and our actors. My heartfelt thanks and admiration to them for making such dedicated and determined mischief.

Erica Whyman, Deputy Artistic Director, June 2014

MIDSUMMER MISCHIEF

FOUR RADICAL NEW PLAYS

The Ant and the Cicada
Timberlake Wertenbaker

Revolt. She said. Revolt again.
Alice Birch

I Can Hear You
E.V. Crowe

This is Not an Exit
Abi Zakarian

OBERON BOOKS
LONDON

WWW.OBERONBOOKS.COM

First published in 2014 by Oberon Books Ltd
521 Caledonian Road, London N7 9RH
Tel: +44 (0) 20 7607 3637 / Fax: +44 (0) 20 7607 3629
e-mail: info@oberonbooks.com
www.oberonbooks.com

A catalogue record for this book is available from the British
Library.

PB ISBN: 978-1-78319-157-4
E ISBN: 978-1-78319-656-2

Cover image: RSC Visual Communications

Printed and bound by Marston Book Services, Didcot.

Visit www.oberonbooks.com to read more about all our books
and to buy them. You will also find features, author interviews and
news of any author events, and you can sign up for e-newsletters
so that you're always first to hear about our new releases.

Contents

THE ANT AND THE CICADA

TIMBERLAKE WERTENBAKER

For Dushka

With thanks to Leda, Demetra, Corinna and Evangelia

Characters

In order of appearance:

SELINA

ALEX

ZOE

IRINA

THE STUDENTS

A Greek island in the present

SCENE 1

Early morning. The front of a dilapidated house, once quite grand. Dry grass, stones. Sense of height and isolation.

SELINA and ALEX come on with heavy suitcases, totally breathless and sweating.

SELINA: This is it. My childhood, my memories, my summers. The cicadas aren't awake yet.

ALEX: *(Breathes heavily.)* You never told me it was so high.

SELINA: Look at the view.

ALEX: Breath-taking.

SELINA: The coast of the Peloponnese is over there, you can't quite see Epidaurus.

ALEX: Is there any water?

SELINA: There used to be a well. Wait here.

ALEX: Couldn't we go into the house?

SELINA goes, ALEX looks around for a moment, amazed but very hot.

ZOE comes out. She stands still and stares at him. She has an old pistol, which she is more or less aiming. She's eccentrically dressed in what might be an old costume.

ZOE: What are you doing here, who are you and what are those cases?

ALEX: *(Easy.)* I thought Greeks were famed for their hospitality.

ZOE: Only to our guests. You look more like an invader.

ALEX: You're the one with the gun. Would it be too much to ask…?

ZOE: It's the shoes. John Lobb. Jermyn Street. You can always judge a man by his shoes. You're not welcome.

ALEX: You must be Zoe. I'm your guest. I mean I'm your sister's guest.

ZOE: Selina!

ALEX: She is your sister?

ZOE: My parents said she was. She's come? Now? After all this time? Where is she?

ALEX: Looking for some water, it was quite a climb. The taxis are on strike. We tried to hire a donkey to carry our luggage but it seems the donkeys are also on strike. I thought the point of being a beast of burden is that you can't withhold your labour. I think Selina tried to explain that to the donkey, I mean the donkey driver, but he just shrugged. The donkey nodded. Although I'm told a nod means no in Greek. We walked up.

ZOE: I take it you don't approve of strikes.

ALEX: I never said that.

ZOE: From your shoes.

ALEX: We were offering very good money. This country is on the brink of starvation but everyone is on strike. Are you on strike?

ZOE: I inconvenience people by working: I'm an artist.

ALEX: Then we're on the same side.

ZOE: That remains to be seen.

ALEX: But you could still lower that pistol.

ZOE: The pistol? Oh, that. It's a prop. Well – it's old.

ALEX: I'm very hot, I don't suppose you have any water?

ZOE: You could take your shoes off, it'll help.

SELINA comes on.

SELINA: The well's filthy, this place is so neglected. Hi, Zoe.

The women kiss, amiably but not warmly.

You've met Alex. I see the old chapel is falling down.

ALEX: Is there a chapel as well?

SELINA: We think it was a temple to Athena, overlaid with a chapel but the roof is caving in. It'll be a ruin soon.

ZOE: The crumbling of centuries of history all in the space of a few years of neglect. An emblem of the current situation. I want to do a performance there.

SELINA: You have the theatre.

ALEX: I'd love to see that.

ZOE: It's only a small amphitheatre, fifteen rows, but on an old model. I had it built myself.

SELINA: The purpose was to get a lot of American students to pay a lot of money to come and study Greek tragedy.

ZOE: That was your idea, Selina, I just wanted an amphitheatre to shout in.

SELINA: I agreed to help if we could put it to some use.

ZOE: We do a lot of shouting these days.

SELINA: You know what I mean, practical use.

ZOE: *(Over.)* Practical. By that you mean the opposite of artistic?

SELINA: Anyway it doesn't matter because the few students who came have stopped coming.

ALEX: Why? It sounds like a great idea. Do you have any bottled water?

ZOE: Greek tragedy doesn't exactly help you get on in life.

SELINA: I'm sure it's the way you presented it.

ZOE: Oedipus and the lessons of leadership? Medea and leaning in? Hecuba and growing old gracefully? Doesn't do it, somehow.

SELINA: *(To ALEX.)* It's this country: American students were afraid because of the strikes and the riots and the murders. And one was found on the rocks down there –

ZOE: *(To ALEX.)* I was hopeless at teaching them, that's all.

ALEX: I would have thought you'd make a good teacher.

ZOE: Not in the morning. Greek tragedies shape themselves around evening violence and they didn't like that. They wouldn't take off their optimism. Which was the reverse side of their fear. I have no patience with fear. I suppose you want some coffee before you go back down?

SELINA: I see you're already on the wine. You're swaying.

ZOE: It's the morning. Events move so fast here it's like history on speed and I try to cling to the previous day before the new day starts. I suppose you check Twitter. 'World under threat.French eat last supper.Greeks go on strike.Merkel blames Med.British blame Bulgarians.Fish blame humans. World ends #Amen'. 140 characters with full stops and no spaces after stops.

SELINA: Why is your phone off?

ZOE: The electricity was cut a month ago, I can't recharge anything unless I go down to the yacht front. The tweets are imaginary but make me feel in touch.

ALEX: What will it take to restore the electricity?

ZOE: You'd have to pay some bills, bribe a few people. Or bribe a lot of people and get hold of a generator. Why?

SELINA: We thought we'd stay for a bit. I tried to tell you but I couldn't get hold of you.

ZOE: Here? No. There's the Poseidon on the sea front, it has five stars and it has its own generator. They'll love Alex's shoes.

SELINA: It's my house too, remember?

ZOE: You're the one who forgets. I've been begging for help. For months.

SELINA: I might be able to help now.

ZOE: *(To Alex.)* There's hardly any water here, you'll be very uncomfortable.

ALEX: I went to public school, nothing makes me uncomfortable, but I am thirsty.

ZOE: Scorpions.

ALEX: My astrological sign. As long as you don't put them in our beds.

ZOE: Beds or bed? I thought you were…

SELINA: We've come to help. I'm sorry it's taken so long –

ZOE: Too long, sister, and maybe too late.

Loud screams not too far away.

ALEX: What's happening?

ZOE: Irina's rehearsing.

More shrieks.

ALEX: What is she rehearsing?

ZOE: Democracy.

SELINA: Wasn't she going to study in England?

ZOE: How? She brings her friends from Athens here. They all want to work with me and learn. We have so many projects – I feed them on olives, ouzo and outrage but even that's running out… Some are coming to the performance tonight – I had to hire boats for them because of the strike.

ALEX: Our boat was very expensive.

SELINA: How are you going to pay?

ZOE: I don't know. That's really why I'm swaying. I don't even know how many are coming.

SELINA: You haven't changed at all, totally impractical, as always. I'm really happy to see you.

The sisters now embrace.

ZOE: You've changed.

SELINA: Me? No. How?

ZOE: I don't know, give me time to study your new mask.

I'll bring out some breakfast.

ALEX: Could I come in and get some water?

ZOE: Stay out here. Enjoy the morning.

ZOE leaves. A silence. The sun is brighter.

SELINA: We're very different, my sister and I. Of course there's the age difference, she's much older. She was my parents' favourite.

Even if she was always in trouble. Like now. Totally self-absorbed and irresponsible. Look at this place.

ALEX: Will she agree?

SELINA: You'll persuade her.

ALEX: What a beautiful place. There's a kind of magic in the light. Didn't you ever want to live here?

SELINA: I hate Greeks.

ALEX: I thought your mother was Greek.

SELINA: I hated my mother. I never understood what she was talking about. And she was such an embarrassment at school. I preferred my father, he did all that unspoken English silence thing brilliantly. He could even rattle Zoe.

ZOE comes back, with food and drink. Lays it down.

ZOE: Coffee, milk, honey, olive oil, yoghurt, cheese, bread, walnuts, wine.

ALEX: Is there – just a glass of water?

SELINA pours and ZOE stays put. A silence. Cicadas start.

It must be difficult to keep up a place like this.

ZOE: I don't keep it up. I keep it. Going. Try – To. Rig the art, navigate the politics or do I mean, rig the politics, navigate…

ALEX: You'll have to keep it up eventually.

ZOE: The olive trees look after themselves more or less. As for the house, it doesn't rain much in Greece.

ALEX: A neglected property soon collapses.

ZOE: Like democracy.

ALEX: Sorry?

ZOE: Neglect it and it collapses. Are you interested in democracy?

ALEX: I'm interested in philosophy.

SELINA: Zoe: Alex wants to help us.

ZOE: You want to help? Does help mean the same thing to you as it does to me?

ALEX: Why wouldn't it?

ZOE: Because it means nothing to Selina.

ALEX: I want to help. For real. Selina told me about this place. I read Greats at University: I've always loved Greece.

ZOE: Ah yes. The idea of Greece. That's very English. But then we get our idea of Greece from you anyway. We're entwined, the Greeks and the English. We invented democracy, you hold it as an idea. If we go down, that idea begins to look very fragile, doesn't it? Yes. You should help. And I should accept. I speak as a Greek here. How do you propose to help?

ALEX: I have some money and I want to – place it here. In Greece.

ZOE: As a tax dodge?

ALEX: I'm looking for something more public.

ZOE: I don't mind. All the Greeks with money are buying property in London. I'm all for a reverse tax dodge.

ALEX: This place is beyond anything Selina described. I'd like to save it. Really.

SELINA: *(To ZOE.)* You see? I couldn't before but I've found a way to help.

ZOE: Last night I went to the chapel and evoked the spirit of Bouboulina. Bouboulina was one of the liberators of Greece when it was under Ottoman rule, we think she took refuge in the chapel. Irina is obsessed with her. Did she hear me? Are you very rich?

ALEX: Yes.

ZOE: May I ask why?

SELINA: Because he's very clever, Zoe.

ALEX: Hedge funds. I have nothing to hide.

ZOE: I've heard of those. You bet against profit and you bet against loss and you never lose.

ALEX: Something like that.

ZOE: So you would bet for and against Greece and win whatever happens?

ALEX: The economy is improving.

ZOE: For the yachts or the donkeys?

SELINA: Zoe, do you want help or not?

ALEX: I happen to be good at finance but it's almost by accident. I never liked it much. But I'm not at ease with English culture either. I don't have a stake in it. I'd like to have a stake in Greece. My first love, let's say.

ZOE: But which Greece? I divide it roughly into four periods: the birth of democracy, that's fifth-century Athens give or take, as you know, the loss of democracy, that's the Ottoman rule, the rebirth of democracy, that's the revolution of 1821 and the crisis of democracy – Right now. Any preferences?

SELINA: He wants to help us, Zoe, not pass a history exam. Why don't you just agree?

ALEX: *(To ZOE.)* I like tragedy.

ZOE: To watch or to join in?

ALEX: I'm in your hands.

ZOE: You could come anytime you wanted and watch our performances. It's not classical tragedy you understand, it's more performance art but it's always about Greece and democracy and yes, you could have a stake. I hope you don't mind working with cash. I have a bank account but there are unpaid taxes. Would you want to help with the performance tonight?

SELINA: Did you say there were unpaid taxes?

ZOE: Of course.

SELINA: How much?

ZOE: A lot I think. Thousands, maybe hundreds of thousands.

SELINA: Why didn't you pay them?

ZOE: How did you expect me to pay them? Anyway, nobody pays their taxes in Greece, you know that. This land and the house have become more and more valuable despite the problems with this country – in fact, it seems, because of the problems. I don't know. I don't want to know. One zero looks like another to me. And they wanted me to pay tax but why should I? I didn't ask for the value to go up. This is our home, these are our olive trees, this house was our grandmother's. A tax inspector came to the island a few months ago and he didn't get past the first cafe before there was a riot. I think he was roughed up a bit and sent back on the boat. He won't be back for a while.

SELINA: You're risking our house.

ZOE: Do you think all those people with yachts down there pay taxes? Anyway, I'm an artist, it's not the sort of thing I think about.

SELINA: There are laws.

ZOE: Don't worry, Selina, they can't get this house, not the tax inspectors. I have protection.

SELINA: There are international laws, Brussels.

ZOE: Oh, Brussels, they're like the Ottoman empire, fat and slow – that's not the problem –

SELINA: The problem is you're in trouble, you have no money, we owe a lot of taxes on this house and Alex is here to help. Can we focus?

ZOE: I am focusing. I'm focusing on the problems of invasion and democracy and national identity. I'm focusing on a local historical heroine called Bouboulina. That's what I do. Focus. But I don't suppose you understand.

SELINA: You always do that to me, don't you? It's what you always did. Tell me I wouldn't understand, I was too little to hear you, too stupid, too narrow-minded. Make me feel inadequate. That mysterious, superior, far away look when you would put on your Creative Face. And you always fooled our parents, didn't you? Even Father. Leave Zoe alone, she's creating, or she's thinking, or she's being interesting, or political. We can all pull out big words and surround them with silence. It's what you always did in your performances. An incomprehensible image or a person very still, for hours. 'Women' a room full of apples and silence. 'Dialogue.' Silence. And that's supposed to explain something. Make the world go around. We're supposed to respect that. Well, no more. You've got yourself into a mess, like the cicada, singing all summer and then she has to go to the ant for help. Remember our mother reciting that? So I've come to help you. You should accept and be grateful.

ZOE: I will be grateful, sister, I will be grateful for any help. Isn't the ant a miser in that fable?

ALEX: Could I go into the house and get some water?

ZOE: Don't mind us. We're sisters. I'm planning a performance about it. The hatred between sisters is unexamined and beyond rationality. It's all the hatred women feel for each other located in two people, close in age, trapped by the same blood, in a world that gives them little space – reduced to the claws of language –

SELINA: *(Over.)* Close in age! Don't flatter yourself. I'm ten years younger than you.

ZOE: That's the problem. You imbibed Thatcherism with your mother's milk.

SELINA: Not from our mother. Anyway, it was bottled.

ZOE: You don't believe in anything except buying and selling. Retail.

SELINA: Oh, please.

ZOE: When our grandmother was interned in a camp as a communist!

SELINA: Here we go…

ALEX: *(Laughs.)* Ladies…Sisters, I mean, I'd like to concentrate on these papers. I want to invest – in this place.

SELINA: In other words, give money to help.

ALEX: But I have to show where my money is going and this document is proof that you agree it's invested here.

ALEX takes out some papers from a case. He's very hot.

I'd love some water.

ZOE: That's a lot of trees you have there. I suppose I have to read it?

SELINA: Don't bother, we can explain it very simply.

ZOE: I don't even read stage directions.

ZOE looks vaguely at the papers and gets immediately very bored.

SELINA: Basically, Alex is offering us money. Which you need.

ZOE: We've already agreed he has a cultural stake in the tragedy that is Greece.

ALEX: This protects my investment.

ZOE: *(Fiddling with the papers.)* What are you afraid of? The cicadas?

SELINA: He's not stupid: Greece is full of Greeks.

ZOE: Is there an amount here? I'd like to know that.

ALEX: It's about 3 million euros.

ZOE: 3 million! You're not serious!

ALEX: I would say that's a third of the value of the property. But we'll have to pay off the taxes. We'll do that for you, don't worry.

SELINA: Sign then.

ZOE: Selina is having you on Alex, the house isn't worth that much. The roof leaks. There isn't really much of a roof, to be truthful. It's almost a ruin.

SELINA: Alex has saved entire companies from ruin – when they got into debt, like you. By the way, how are you going to pay for the boats tonight?

ZOE: Some people agreed to help.

SELINA: Yacht people?

ZOE: Of course not. It doesn't matter, it's complicated – I'd rather they didn't.

ALEX: If you need cash I can get it to you by tomorrow.

ZOE: How much? We may have as many as thirty students. That's four or five boats.

ALEX: I can get you whatever you want. Three hundred thousand in cash?

ZOE: Three hundred thousand? 3 Million. All those zeros for a stake in tragedy?

ALEX: *(Smiling.)* What price tragedy?

ZOE: *(Smiles.)* Selina's always had such elegant taste in men.

SELINA: A stake has to be legally signed for.

ZOE: I still don't understand…

ALEX: Because of the land really.

ZOE: The olive grove. It's in the guide books but it's hardly worth –

ALEX: Land is always complicated.

ZOE: But if I sign, does the house somehow belong to the three of us? It's our family house, you understand.

ALEX: You keep the full use of the house. It's all in here.

SELINA: You've said yourself you don't believe in ownership. It won't make much difference, we're not going to live here. You know that.

ZOE: Can I think about it?

SELINA: What is there to think about? Anyway, you shouldn't try to think when you've been drinking.

ZOE: I could wait till I'm sober.

ALEX: That would delay paying for the boats. Or anything else.

ZOE: There are a few urgent debts…

SELINA: And so, sign. You can have cash now. You can have your performance. You're signing the salvation of our property. Have another glass of wine, let's celebrate.

ZOE: When you were little, I used to threaten you with terrible punishments if you betrayed me.

SELINA: You never even told me what they were but I was so afraid I never did betray you, did I? I wouldn't have anyway because you were my big sister and even though you generally ruined my life, I loved you and admired you. You know it's the only solution. You need the money. Irina can keep shrieking. And you'll have this house, our childhood house, our memories, our summers.

ZOE: It's even more than that. It's democracy. If you knew – but yes. You're right. I'll sign. Now. Can you hear the cicadas?

She drinks. She signs. Shrieks from IRINA.

SCENE 2

Late afternoon. ZOE is working on a cage made with bamboo and twine and the cloth of a Greek flag. ALEX comes on.

ALEX: I'm not used to sleeping in the middle of the day.

ZOE: This is my favourite time. Five o'clock in the afternoon. *And the bull alone exultant. A las cinco de la tarde. Bones and flutes ring in his ears, a las cinco de la tarde…*

ALEX: Isn't that Spanish?

ZOE: Lorca was a Greek in spirit. Bullfights must have started in Greece.

ALEX: I hate bullfights.

ZOE: You like your violence more subtle and well-cooked. Sort of supermarket violence?

ALEX: More a sense of fair play. The bull always dies.

ZOE: The bull has to die because he represents brutal and untrammelled force. He's outwitted by the little effeminate bullfighter, it's very hopeful. Do you like this cage? It's for tonight.

ALEX: Are you playing Bouboulina?

ZOE: Irina is Bouboulina. I'm playing Greece or maybe Democracy – it's a performance piece and so there's an image, some guidelines and then we see what happens. The Greek flag is beautiful, don't you think? These nine stripes represent the nine letters of freedom in Greek or some say the nine muses. And the cross here represents a crossroads – the crux of Greek tragedy – standing at the crossroads…

ALEX: Who goes in the cage?

ZOE: I think I start in there and then I suppose the Ottomans go in there when Bouboulina has done her revolution stuff.

What's interesting is that when people see you through bars, even a few bamboo pieces, you lose all the trappings of your power. Do you want to try it?

ALEX: Not really.

ZOE: There are all kinds of stripteases with women in cages. It's very sexy, it seems. Shall I show you?

ALEX: It's not my sort of thing, Zoe.

ZOE: And then a bamboo cage probably ended the war in Vietnam. Remember?

ALEX: I was a pimply scholarship boy studying Greek.

ZOE: American Might suddenly looked vulnerable with Marines in a cage. The image told you the war was going to be lost. But now, if we both go in the cage, it becomes intimate and protective. Come. We're bound together, skin to skin, side by side, looking out or looking in. I find you incredibly attractive.

ALEX: I'm not sure what I'm supposed to say to that.

ZOE: You have a choice, call it a crossroads. You can move towards me and we can see if our skins really like each other, you never know, I like the colouring of yours but the feel will be the test – or you can recoil because I've frightened you with my directness. There's a possibility you don't feel any attraction of course but at five o'clock in the afternoon, everything is attraction.

ALEX: *(Moving towards her.)* You are…

ZOE: And I have a choice. I can move another step towards you and savour the attraction of skin or…I can check those stage directions I didn't bother to read.

ALEX: I think the stage directions would say that we move towards each other.

ZOE: The breeze of the late afternoon, the rustle of the olive trees, the tired heat of the day.

ALEX: Greece. A powerful and beautiful woman with long wild hair.

ZOE: The stranger bearing gifts.

ALEX: So then…

ZOE: The cicadas sing…even the industrious ant stops to listen. Where's Selina?

ALEX: I think she's gone down into the town.

ZOE: Why?

ALEX: Socrates says somewhere that desire is always the desire for something we lack. I've only now understood what he meant. Something here, in you, reminds me that I turned one way – made the money – enjoyed that power – and forgot – lacked – call it the complexity of response – But now – here –

ZOE: You're not in love with my sister?

ALEX: We're business partners. I like her.

ZOE: Do you know her well? What a stupid question. Who knows anyone well?

ALEX: I'd like to know you better. I like artists. I feel more at ease with them. I was going that way until I discovered I had this odd talent for making money. But I've done that now and I have other things…I wouldn't mind translating a tragedy if you needed one.

ZOE: I didn't quite explain that the performance tonight is about modern Greece. Well, Greece in 1821. It ends in freedom. That's not tragic if you stop at the right time. About 1824. And now it's my turn to define desire, a *Greek* poet this time: *soma, thimisou oxi mono poso agapithikes…body remember not only how much you were loved, not only the beds on which you lay, but also those desires for you that glowed plainly in the eyes…*

ALEX: Still do…

ZOE: It takes words now…not just skin.

ALEX: All the more attractive.

ZOE: *(After a moment.)* It should be so easy…

ALEX: Nothing to stop us.

ZOE: Do you know how you become aware that there's about to be an earthquake in Greece? The cicadas stop singing. The cicadas know this in some way –

ALEX: *(Closer.)* I can hear the cicadas, Zoe.

ZOE: I don't think they stop because they're psychic, I think they stop because the earth sounds different. And the sound of this place has been different all afternoon. It can't be just because you want to translate a Greek tragedy.

ALEX: I have a modern play as well. A play I've written. It's very funny. I think it could be quite successful. It's about truth and lying.

ZOE: Words and words reversed? Can you tell the difference?

ALEX: Will you look at it? I'd love your opinion. I thought it could be tried here. Maybe you could get your students –

ZOE: It's the islanders who come and watch us. Not many speak English.

ALEX: I mean, when we have an English audience.

ZOE: People on yachts think seeing a fish is epic drama.

ALEX: When the English come here. Friends… I can invite some producers.

ZOE: Where's the contract, Alex?

ALEX: I think Selina has it.

ZOE: Tell me exactly what I signed?

ALEX: No more than what we explained. The house and the land become a company. We are the three directors.

ZOE: And I'm the artistic dictator. I mean, director.

ALEX: Exactly and we manage the finances for you. We pay for the boats but also for the students.

ZOE: You'll pay them as well? They'll be thrilled, some of them won't have eaten.

ALEX: They can have cash tonight. Travel expenses, a little extra, would 200 Euros do?

ZOE: They'll be amazed. And there's Irina. Even if she is my daughter. She has the shrieking part and shrieking is as much of an effort as speaking, believe me.

ALEX: 500 Euros for her? A thousand if you like.

ZOE: I could fall into your arms I'm so grateful. Actually, I've wanted to fall into your arms since you first came but every time…something…a shift in sound –

ALEX: I hear only the breeze…

ZOE: When you spend months alone you learn to listen – a cracking branch – a sudden disturbance – here it is:

SELINA comes on.

SELINA: The paths have got impossible. We'll have to fix them. I lost my way.

ZOE: That's the point. What were you doing down in the town?

SELINA: I went to look at the Poseidon, as you suggested. We could go now.

ZOE: Aren't you watching the performance?

SELINA: It's not one of your long things is it? Did you say you were doing Bouboulina? Didn't you do it years ago?

ZOE: That was the children's version.

SELINA: You forced me to play a vicious jellyfish.

ZOE: Viscous actually. It suited you. What were you doing in town?

SELINA: I gave the contracts to Stavros.

ZOE: Stavros? He's a crook.

SELINA: He told me something very disturbing, Zoe. He said you'd been seen talking to members of Golden Dawn.

ZOE: You can't talk to any man around here without gossip. They'll be saying we're engaged in a threesome before you know it.

SELINA: But why would you have any conversations with Golden Dawn? Why would they come up here? They're fascists, right? We had a grandmother in the camps, right?

ZOE: What do you mean by fascists?

SELINA: A fascist is a fascist, Zoe, don't do words on me. I read the papers, they hate immigrants. They beat them up in Athens.

ZOE: Well, they also beat up the tax inspector. That was a good thing or you wouldn't have a house left.

SELINA: We'll have nothing to fear from tax inspectors from now on.

ZOE: That's great: I won't have to talk to Golden Dawn anymore.

SELINA: Have to?

ZOE: A form of words. Necessity if you like, you know, like the goddess: Necessity.

SELINA: No I don't know. I don't do Greek goddesses.

ZOE: What cannot be resisted. (*To ALEX.*) The Greek Goddess Ananke.

ALEX: My father was an immigrant. He was beaten up occasionally. I was beaten up at school. Although maybe not for being an immigrant's son but for being very clever. What was the necessity if I may ask?

ZOE: I told you: the tax inspector, the whole thing. Those who wanted to get me out. I only talked to them a few times. They're running half the island anyway.

ALEX: I didn't know that.

ZOE: They're not interested in skin colour, believe me. They have food banks.

SELINA: What did they want in return?

ZOE: They were happy to get one over the bureaucrats and financiers. They hate global finance and what's happened to Greece, which is something I can sympathise with.

SELINA: Out with it.

ZOE: They wanted to hold a couple of meetings here. In the amphitheatre.

SELINA: A meeting? A fascist meeting?

ZOE: Alex wants to do a play here, I'm not saying no just because I think it's going to be terrible. If they want a meeting, where they talk, what's wrong with that?

SELINA: A fascist meeting on our grandmother's land?

ZOE: She was a communist, not a saint. They have MPs in government. They're voted in. That's democracy, you don't get what you want but you get some of it, you tolerate the rest.

SELINA: You've betrayed everything our grandmother fought for. She'll be turning in her grave and sending curses through the earth.

ZOE: You're becoming very Greek suddenly. Have an ouzo. We should think about supper. I don't suppose you did any shopping in town? No, you never do. The students will be here soon. We'll perform with the full moon. I can probably find some eggs. Or a chicken if you're really hungry. Or a cat.

ALEX: I saw some chickpeas when I was in the kitchen. I'll make us a soup.

He leaves.

SELINA: My Greek sister! A fascist.

ZOE: It's easy to be liberal when you have enough to eat.

SELINA: Aren't you ashamed? All your sermons, I mean your performances: love, tolerance, the feminine mystics.

ZOE: I think you mean the feminine mystique.

SELINA: Whatever. Non-violence. You did a bloody workshop on it. You made me act the policeman with a truncheon. I was only 8 and all your friends shouted and called me a fascist pig. I thought I was supposed to be Piglet in Winnie the Pooh. I was totally confused. What's happened to you?

ZOE: All right. I'm blushing. I was desperate. They're not very bright and I thought I could handle them. I had to save the house. For us. The past. And for Irina. The future. Your niece. Your blood. Our DNA. The only one of the next generation…who needs this inheritance. Maybe it matters less to you because – I'm sorry – I know –

SELINA: *(Angry.)* Leave it!

A silence. It's an awkward subject. Cicadas.

ZOE: I think I'm falling in love. The last one was a composer but he had a stuntman in the background and I couldn't compete. Who's Alex's stuntman?

SELINA: Three teenage children.

ZOE: I could handle that. Why haven't you done anything? He's closer to you in age, he's charming.

SELINA: *(Shrugs.)* I'm not attracted to artists.

ZOE: He isn't one but anyway, it's not like taking drugs, or being a thief. It may seem so to you, but it really isn't. It's to do with the future, singing for the future. Like the cicadas. To procreate. Even if it's only other cicadas. The Greeks loved cicadas because they thought they just appeared, from the earth and fed on air, singing for free. The science is wrong but the metaphor is right. The sound of continuity, the future, desire. Listen.

SELINA: I have no desire.

ZOE: Sometimes I'm ashamed of mine. The gap between orgasms and Alzheimer's narrows by the day. But you? What's happened?

SELINA: I don't know. Nothing means much. I'm tired. It's not retail by the way, it's marketing.

ZOE: Sorry, what's the difference?

SELINA: It's the difference between the thing and the package. Improving the appeal appeal by establishing a dialogue with the public. It's extremely complex and subtle actually. And competitive.

ZOE: That's what it is. Your face. You've improved it.

SELINA: Only a little, around the eyes.

ZOE: I can't read it anymore. Why do it?

SELINA: Because everyone else does it. Because that's the market. You wouldn't understand. That's why I thought I'd come here. To renew myself. Have a project.

ZOE: I'm glad you're here. Most of the time I want to kill you because you're my sister but sometimes I want to envelop you with tenderness because you're my sister and if I can hold you, in this moment, in this golden afternoon, nothing will change, nothing will disappear.

SELINA moves away.

SELINA: I suppose I should have explained more clearly. It's about the property.

ZOE: We can repair the roof now.

SELINA: That's not enough. And so I discussed it with Alex.

ZOE: He's been with me all afternoon. Not in that way – I got distracted. Well, there's tonight. As long as you don't mind. Actually, it would be more fun if you did mind.

SELINA: You don't really want to know, do you?

ZOE: Do you know what my students hated most about Greek tragedy? The inability of the protagonists to see what is right in front of them. They found it wilful.

SELINA: They're right, it's intensely irritating.

ZOE: It's because the hero always hears a different language. And then the chorus usually goes into a seemingly irrelevant song and dance. Remember when we used to practice Greek dances together to impress the Greek boys? When Greece stood for sensuality and insouciance? Come on – I want to recover some joy for you.

ZOE takes SELINA into the beginning of a standard Greek dance.

It's not your health is it? I couldn't bear to lose you.

SELINA: It might as well be now when you're quite drunk. You must know – that when you signed the papers –

ZOE: Try speaking from the cage –

ZOE forces SELINA to the cage. ALEX comes on.

I'm really very non-violent but sometimes I forget.

SELINA: Can you explain our plans to Zoe?

ALEX: Now? The chickpeas are cooking.

ZOE: The cicadas are singing. They stop. The messenger comes on. He never has good news.

ALEX: This isn't bad news at all, Zoe. We've invested in this property. That is, I have since I've put up the money, those millions you're so happy about. Selina and you have sold me a share in your property. But I'm a businessman.

ZOE: You can't be a businessman and write plays, Alex, it's like trying to stand in the middle of the crossroads without ever moving.

ALEX: I'll want a return on my investment. It's only natural.

ZOE: I didn't know investments were part of the natural world.

ALEX: I studied the plans Selina brought me.

ZOE: There are no plans.

SELINA: The land is registered, even in Greece. I got hold of the plans.

ZOE: Without telling me.

SELINA: You didn't tell me about the fascists.

ALEX: And my idea is that you could make a huge return by developing the land. What we have in mind is to build a complex. Nothing high obviously, that wouldn't be allowed although all the planning permissions are out the window at the moment. Greek style, spreading around various courtyards, with walls for privacy. Very safe for the Russian Oligarchs. Private for the Chinese. And there are more and more English now with real money. Water's not a problem because you have a well. A swimming pool, tasteful of course, a couple of tennis courts. I want to emphasise something high end, cultural, Greek yachts have become common – and that's where the theatre comes in. A place for international conferences as well. Sort of Davos by the sea. It could work very well. We would build on the land over there.

ZOE: That's where the olive trees are. Sorry. The olive trees are sacred.

SELINA: To whom?

ZOE: To Athena for one. To our grandmother. To me. That's the one thing I've looked after. You're eating the olives right now. Sometimes I barter them.

Shrieks.

Irina's warming up – I'd love to accommodate your plans but the olive trees are in the way.

SELINA: You have to live in the real world, Zoe.

ZOE: What is the real world, Selina?

SELINA: Well, not the world of childhood memories and endless summers. The world that pays you to sing. No one wants that anymore. Or you.

You've lived on subsidies all your life. In England first and when they dried up, you came here. And now that's gone and you ask yourself why. But why should we subsidize you? Just give you money. What do you have to offer? At least in London theatre attracts tourists and pays for itself. But it doesn't here unless it's Epidaurus. We're offering you a good way out. The property will be put to good use, you'll have money, you can do what you want. You can travel.

ZOE: Drift around hotel rooms like a character from *The Cherry Orchard*?

SELINA: We're talking about some ugly old olive trees. Who said anything about a cherry orchard.

ZOE: It's a play.

SELINA: I know it's a play. I saw it.

ZOE: You went to *The Cherry Orchard*?

SELINA: There was someone from Woody Allen: I thought it'd be a romcom about getting married –

ZOE: That's one interpretation of it.

SELINA: Anyway, I hated it: those people are history.

ZOE: Well done: yes, the play was written before the Russian Revolution.

SELINA: I don't mean that kind of history. I mean toast history. History as toast.

ZOE: Sorry? Is that a new academic discipline?

SELINA: All those Russians drifting about being depressed and remembering their childhood, listening to the cicadas or the mosquitoes or whatever. All despising the ants. Who work. Who work hard. Who make the world go round. Who are supposed to feel guilty about it. And pay others to make nice sounds. The sounds are different now. And actually, I think people quite like the new sound. People like Alex and me. Who keep the world afloat. Who pay for everything. Who are real.

ZOE: Real? Who said you were real?

ALEX: What we're saying is that we are realists. This is really the only solution if you want to keep your house.

ZOE: You said you really wanted to help.

ALEX: I am helping but as Selina says, we have to live in the real world. And the real world is economic.

ZOE: Is it? There's an advantage to being old and that's that you remember other languages before they went extinct. In most cultures, that's the responsibility of women. That's why they're hated: the language furies.

I've listened to people like you work at wiping out the language over the last forty years. The new words come in, like some new species that proliferates and suppresses the native ones. You've convinced us that we aren't human, but economic entities. And when we say equality, fairness, security, you say we're preaching sentiment but you're the ones who are preaching except it that it's new and sort of sexy.

When I was at uni economics was tagged on after politics, philosophy.

And then one day, you were all over the place like an evangelical horde, trampling philosophy and politics in your wake. And you brought your God. A very male God. A God as testosterone-filled, unpredictable and cruel as the God of the Old Testament with his chosen people. And

as delusional as the God of the New Testament, promising
a beatific afterlife. Suffer now, tighten your belt, take the
difficult decision and economic heaven is around the
corner. For the saved of course, never mind the others.
Martyr yourselves to the economy that it may resurrect.
How different is that from angels or grapes and virgins in
Paradise?

And you've brought in the kind of terror they wouldn't
have even thought possible in the middle ages. If we
protest, refuse unemployment, kids in despair, hunger,
the wrath of the market will bear down on us. Protest is
blasphemy. Your God is a jealous God.

Words that were former friends become traitors: altruism?
You might as well worship Athena if you believe in
altruism. It can only be reciprocal altruism: nothing for
nothing. Fairness? In your constructed universe life just
isn't fair. Your language closes all questioning.

But you know, when people withdrew their worship
from Athena and Zeus, the world didn't collapse. It turns
out they didn't really exist. And when some people said
God was dead, hell didn't break loose. And maybe your
universe doesn't exist either and your prophets invent
their prophecies like all the other prophets before them. It
may be the world you've created is just that, a creation. No
more real than anything else.

What would happen if we liberated all the words you've
taken hostage? Like choice. That was a great achievement.
I can choose what kind of shoes I want but I can't choose
to have them. A Fact is what you dictate. And when a
word is uncomfortable, like art, you change it to creative
industry, an ant word.

But your prize hostage is Democracy. Democracy can
only exist if it obeys god the market. Your irrational and
capricious god. Challenge the market, democracy will
collapse, so you say.

Democracy is supposed to give power to people but if
people only ever hear your economic language, where's

the power? How can there be democracy if there are no words to think with?

SELINA: Are you finished?

ZOE: Yes. I'm finished. What I'm trying to tell you is that I won't allow you to build on the olive grove. Have some Retsina.

ALEX: There's one difficulty there, Zoe.

ZOE: Really? A difficult decision maybe? That's another economism.

ALEX: The company is owned by three directors.

ZOE: Yes and I'm one of them.

ALEX: The structure is democratic. Decisions are taken by a majority vote. It's in the contract. We outnumber you.

ZOE: So those were the hidden stage directions…

But Selina would never vote against me. Would you?

A silence.

Give me back the contract.

ALEX: You may despise my world but in my world, a contract is a contract.

ZOE: A contract is something you understand.

ALEX: Sorry but it's something you sign. It's up to you to have understood it.

ZOE: I won't accept that.

ALEX: It's for the best: why would you want to be poor when you don't have to?

ZOE: *(To SELINA.)* This is a betrayal.

SELINA: *(Kind.)* I had to save you – and us. It was – necessary – Please don't cry.

ZOE: *You think I'll weep?…no I'll not weep. I will do such things… what they are…*

SELINA: There's nothing you can do. Or is that from something? I never know…

ZOE: Only some old tragic words about revenge. Was this yours, Selina? Because I warn you: in a tragedy, everyone loses. There are the students coming up the hill. We have to get the performance ready.

SCENE 3

Evening. IRINA appears in full gear as BOUBOULINA: gorgeous costume and pistols.

BOUBOULINA: My name is Laskarina Bouboulina. I'm an historical character. We are in 1821. I am fighting for Greek freedom against the Ottoman Empire. I could use a lot of dramatic dialogue to tell you the same thing but there's no time to lose.

Greece at the time of the Ottomans is multi-ethnic and multicultural and rather tolerant. There's choice. But there is one big problem. Bureaucracy. The Turkish yoke, as the Greeks call it, is a bureaucratic yoke operated by a rich and powerful class of money lenders and administrators, that is bankers and tax collectors, known for their corruption and lack of pity. Well, they usually go together. Most Greeks, those we like to patronize as 'ordinary people,' are reduced to subsistence living because of the taxes and the corruption. That's the end of the history lesson. What you have to imagine is an island like this, with people working desperately hard to get enough to eat. People submit to the terror of the future and say little. Sort of like now but with costumes.

Two students come on in 'poor' costumes, vaguely Balkan.

The Greece I'm fighting for is partly your invention, you the English who are here, that is. You've turned a sleepy Balkan country under relatively benign Islamic rule into an emblem of Western liberty. You create a new country out an old word: democracy. You conceive a cradle and put the baby, the new Greece, into it. And that baby is to grow up and spawn a lot of children, your own democracies. Emblematically. You love the Parthenon but unlike the Elgin marbles, it can't fit into the British museum and

35

so the next best thing is to liberate it and then invade it yourselves.

So here you are, the English speakers in the audience, implicated, godparents as it were, and I need you to be active. Very active. As in: audience participation active. Don't panic. You won't have to get on stage. Not now anyway. You only need to prepare.

The parts are divided in two: historical characters and characters with tendencies. Let's call them the Hists and the Ists-Ist as in Humanist, Fascist. There are other characters too. This will all become clear as we go along. We also have thirty students ready to rush on when we need them but the two we have here will come around shortly and be generally helpful.

I, Bouboulina, am the main historical character and like all historical characters in theatre, I have a real past life, a symbolic life and a present life. All superimposed like layers in rock. I live in several times. I'm anachronistic. Anyone here hate anachronisms? You can fill in a complaint form later. Try to accept it for now. The past never disappears and it's on stage that you can weld it to the present, joining the different times like different metals.

1821. Greece revolts but the words are sung by an English poet, Lord Byron. So we start with Hists. Some of you have just agreed to take a card. Like most decisions this one will have unpredictable consequences. If you have a card with the letter B, please raise it. You're Byrons.

THE STUDENT: *The isles of Greece! The isles of Greece!*
Where burning Sappho loved and sung,
Where grew the arts of war and peace,

BOUBOULINA: The students are coming around with a few lines to inspire you and you can have a sweet while you're at it. If you already know some Byron or if you have wavy hair or a brooding look, we have some extra Bs. You can also trade with your neighbour. All you need to do is be intense, Hellenic, idealistic, Apollonic. I have a wig if you want more hair.

Then we need another English poet, Percy Bysshe Shelley. Where are the S's? You have to be radical and rebellious. If this comes naturally to you, take an extra S card.

THE STUDENT: *Faiths and empires gleam*
Like wrecks of a dissolving dream.

BOUBOULINA: We've got the whole poem here but it's very long and fairly obscure. You only need to remember a few words from its preface and say, whenever you feel like it: *We are all Greeks.* Got it? *We are all Greeks.*

THE STUDENT: *Alas! For Liberty!*

BOUBOULINA: Tonight, I, Bouboulina, from this island, will try to free Greece. I'll do it violently because I have no choice. It will mean killing and suffering for women and children because that's what always happens.

THE STUDENT: *And ravening Famine left his ocean cave*
To dwell with war, with us and with despair

BOUBOULINA: I have ships. I have money from some dead husbands and a Russian, Count Stroganov, who I think is also responsible for Beef Stroganov. Those with C cards are my crew. Where are you? I need more than that. Anyone good at sailing? Passionate about freedom? I have pistols here, loaded, and a grenade or two. I will personally command a ship called the Agamemnon. Here are pictures of the ship for the crew, a few instructions on naval battles as well as some rations of ouzo to fortify you.

We're now ready to mix in the present. So: a new yoke strangles Greece. Call it the global economic yoke: bureaucrats, bankers, traders and tax collectors, corrupt and without pity.

You may not know this but the first king of modern Greece was Otto, the son of a Bavarian King. The Greeks were busy arguing about freedom and so he took over. We've always had an interesting relationship with the Germans. Who has an M? You're Angela Merkel. It's a great part. Not much comedy in it but you get respect and sensible clothes. We have some speeches but we didn't have time to translate them and they're still in German.

ZOE appears.

Here is my mother. She's a bit Greek and a bit English. *We are all Greeks*. Remember? *We are all Greeks*.

She's going to face a moral dilemma. Anyone here good at moral dilemmas? Who has an H card? You're humanists.

THE STUDENT: ...*I believe that the foundations for ethics and society are to be found in autonomy and moral equality*...

BOUBOULINA: You can improvise the rest. You need to look human and have some ideas. My mother is a woman and so I'll need some feminists. Those are the FM cards, not to be confused with the FS cards for Fascists and the FB cards for Fabulists. What do the feminists have to do? Be confident, decisive but not bossy. Be idealistic, realistic, linguistic. Beware the strident tendency. You can talk but not talk too much. Exhibit acute listening skills.

If you're not at ease with your part and your neighbour won't trade, practise empathy. We have exercise cards if you need help.

There should be an OFS or two. That's an Old-Fashioned Socialist. You have to mumble and look sort of embarrassed as if the rug had been pulled from under you. The Blairists are all abroad. Where are the Fascists? I know twenty members of Golden Dawn are here. UK for Ukip? Now for Es. You're the economists. Act knowledgeable, secure, mathematical and well-fed. Look as if you know how to get us out of the mess you've got us into. Is there anyone here who is or would like to be called Robert Peston? We have the specs. Piketty? You can tell us in the bar how the rich get richer but for now, just act French. The students will help you.

The students do a French shrug.

THE STUDENT: Capital –

THE STUDENT: isme

BOUBOULINA: Those of you who have decided it's time for a change can join me Bouboulina as Bouboulinists.

THE STUDENT: *The world is weary of the past –*

Oh, might it die or rest at last!

BOUBOULINA: Where are the Oligarchists? That's basically someone who believes that power should be concentrated in the hands of the few, preferably close friends. Oligarchs? You get to have fun and ignore the future. But our students will find it difficult to help you. Any real oligarchs who could advise? Let me rephrase that: anyone here with disproportionate wealth?

I haven't forgotten the moral dilemma. I will now ask you to do something we always try to do in any performance. Bring yourselves, as you are, into your parts. If that's too difficult, just be yourselves. We're going to start with a traditional hostage taking.

The students bring ALEX on who is reluctant and embarrassed.

You take a hostage when there is no way else to get anyone to listen. Or when you're in desperate need of money. This man is our hostage. He has an accomplice.

The student leads SELINA.

I'm going to give my mother a gun.

She gives ZOE a gun.

The gun is loaded. From what I know of my mother, she is capable of using it.

ZOE: I have always believed in non-violence. Peaceful sit-ins, demonstrations, all that. But my beliefs have never really been put to the test. How good is a belief that doesn't work? At what point is violence the only resort?

BOUBOULINA: I told you she wasn't good at the moral dilemma. Consider now who you are and where you stand. If you're confused, you can act the chorus and waver from side to side. Or you can just repeat: we are all Greeks. We are all Greeks. We are all Greeks.

The hostage who stands here has plans to develop and sell off this land, in other words, turn it into a commodity. All you need to know about commodities is that they don't benefit the commodity itself.

THE STUDENT: *For Greeks a blush – for Greece a tear.*

BOUBOULINA: These two signed a contract with my mother. But she didn't understand the contract. Is there anyone here who still thinks people are basically nice and happy to give up power if you only reason with them? That's my mother.

ZOE: Who can resist the hand that offers help for nothing? Why not believe in that? I didn't know that the definition of human beings as capable of giving doesn't exist anymore. In the economic world we have created, giving for nothing makes no sense. But if I didn't know that, am I bound by my contract?

BOUBOULINA: What do you think?

THE STUDENT: *What? Silent still and silent all?*

ALEX is very still. SELINA annoyed.

ZOE: I'm asking you to relinquish the contract. If you won't relinquish the contract, I may have to shoot you.

BOUBOULINA: When is violence justified? When is it inevitable?

THE STUDENT: *Must we but blush? – Our fathers bled.*

BOUBOULINA: Who would like a gun? We have lots. Of course, why worry about Greece at all? Because Greece is you. Remember? *We are all Greeks. We are all Greeks.*

ZOE: Will you relinquish the contract?

ALEX thinks this is a joke, tries to get away and is stopped. ZOE turns to SELINA.

You may be my sister but you betrayed me. Relinquish the contract.

SELINA hesitates.

BOUBOULINA: Does the social contract trump the economic contract? There she stands, my mother. I say to her: occupy. Where are the Activists?

THE STUDENT: *….a new race has arisen throughout Europe…and she will continue to produce fresh generations to accomplish the destiny which tyrants foresee and dread…*

ZOE: How long would an occupying movement last? A week, a few months? But what's called the forces of order in the Orwellian language of economics would come and create a riot. No. The brute force of the bull has to be outwitted.

BOUBOULINA: My mother identifies with bullfighters. No, I don't ask. Sometimes she thinks she's a cicada although she knows those who sing are male. But then I'm Bouboulina and I'm supposed to be minding the crockery instead of misbehaving on an historical scale.

ZOE: An image has no gender. The cicadas sing to procreate. They make the future. We sing to procreate. We believe in the future. We can't help ourselves. If we sing, there might be a future. We say: let us sing. You don't need us but the future might. That's what we say.

BOUBOULINA: It's simple for me, Bouboulina. It's a war of liberation. It needs violence. I wave a flag. It's more difficult for her, now, in the twenty-first century. What's the war? What's the liberation?

ZOE: It's always a liberation of language. The tragic gesture liberates the language for a moment. A voice cries out for the old laws of burial, for the just rules of the house-oikonomos-economy. The one who didn't see in time mourns in public. The one betrayed rages and revenges. We are all those voices. A voice that curses the economic picture of the world as no more accurate than those old maps with dragons. The voice that speaks out for a brief moment before it is silenced again. The fear that you feel at the end of a tragedy is the silence that follows.

BOUBOULINA: Greece, under the bureaucratic yoke of the Ottoman Empire was silent for four hundred years. Bouboulina, having fought for liberation with her own ships and guns was shot in a family dispute. The Greeks fall silent.

ZOE: Sometimes in the remote hills of some forgotten island you hear a high-pitched shriek.

IRINA shrieks.

BOUBOULINA: Democracy.

ZOE: But mostly there is silence.

BOUBOULINA: Or violence.

ZOE and BOUBOULINA aim at SELINA and ALEX.

ZOE: Until the words reshape themselves. Once again.

REVOLT. SHE SAID. REVOLT AGAIN.

ALICE BIRCH

For my Mum.
The first revolutionary I knew

It wouldn't have come out the way it has without many women,
but namely:

Susan Brownmiller

Helen Goalen and Abbi Greenland

Nina Power

Valerie Solanas

Erica Whyman

I want to thank the RSC – Mark, Claire, Réjane, Collette,
Pippa and Sarah

Giles
and Sam.

Consider the idea that offstage should be as visible to the audience as possible. 'The actors' are another set of characters. Shoes – particularly high ones – should be taken off and on, lipstick removed and reapplied. If any vomiting, crying or shouting needs to happen offstage, the audience should be able to glimpse it at the very least.

There shouldn't be any set. The play should be performable without any props.

Ideally, the play should be performed by a cast of six.

There should be at least one female character (that should probably be played by a female actor) in every scene.

If a woman has to get a bit naked at any point, then the men should get naked also to redress the balance.

A dash – indicates a change of speaker.

/ Denotes the overlapping of speech.

Words in square brackets [ ] are not spoken.

The absence of a full stop at the end of a line denotes a kind of interruption – the lines should run at speed.

The use of a full stop on a line on its own suggests a pause – whether this is a single beat or ten minutes depends on what feels right.

The spacing of the dialogue, the use of upper and lower case letters and the punctuation is all there to help the actor in terms of the pacing and the weight of their words.

If the titles are shown, in Act Two they should stack up on top of one another in some way.

Most importantly, this play should not be well behaved.

Act One

REVOLUTIONIZE THE LANGUAGE. (INVERT IT.)

–   I don't understand.

        .

        I don't understand how you do what you do to me.

–   I don't Do anything to you.

        I Don't.

        I do

        Whatever I do

        And whatever You think or feel or

        Whatever

        Is all you – is All you.

–   I want to make love to you.

        You are a Brilliant Bright Bright thing – do you have any idea what your shoulders, bare like that, do to me, do to my structure, to my insides – I want to make a brooch out of your hair and your pupils and your ribs – and I know that sounds fucking – but I want to pin that to my heart and let my blood drain I'm done it's You let's Everybody Out Now World I Am Gone.

        .

        I bought you bluebells.

        I made him wrap them – I had the little man wrap them in brown paper for you – I want – and I have been thinking – All Day Long

        That I want to make love to you – don't move, don't move, just for a second just
could you stay exactly where you are?

–   I

–   You look completely perfect

–   Can I

–   You look completely and utterly perfect – stay exactly
      as you are

      .

–   Can I just

      put this down?

–   No

–   Are you – ?

–   It's your body – it's the line of your body

–   Yeah, but can I

–   It's the line your neck makes

–   Makes?

–   Your hip, there like that

–   It's just my / hip

–   / Is perfection

–   I'm just.

      I'm going to move now

      Because there's all this [mess] to clear up and.

–   You're perfection.

–   What's that [noise] – is that a

–   Perfection

–   Nightingale or a

–   Complete Perfection

–   Wine? Do you want wine?

–   All through dinner, all I could think about was getting
      you home and making love to you – the only thought
      in my head, the whole way through that fucking cheese
      course was That mole
      on your jaw
      and how I wanted to lick it.

–   You ate loads of cheese

–   I was thinking about licking your mole

–   You ate an Enormous amount of cheese – I was
beginning to feel Worried, I was considering Expressing
Concern – you physically Put me off cheese, I could
barely finish my watermelon – d'you want a drink or

–   I can barely hear what you're saying – I'm obsessed – I
barely heard a word Anyone said – all I could think
about was fucking you

–   They were talking about North Korea

–   Your lips. That lip.

–   Over cheese. I thought you were really into it, I thought
you were really Absorbed –
you looked – they were talking about prison camps and
Genocide – about Mass
Genocide – you looked. You Looked Moved.

–   All I could think about was coming home, laying you
down upon that bed

–   That bit about that family who'd had all their fingers
cut off, I thought

–   Thinking about you and

–   I thought you were were Welling Up

–   Laying you down upon that bed
And making love to you.

–   .

–   And making love to you

–   .

–   Laying you down. And making love to you.

–   Or

–   No or

–   Or

–   There Is no Or – there is no other option

–   Yes but

–   I want to make Love to you

–   Or

        With?

–   .

        With.

        With.

        .

        With you – make love – I want to make love With you

–   Yeah?

–   Yeah

–   Yeah

–   Yes

–   Aaaaand?

–   And, yes, and and kissing you, I want to kiss you –
        With you, I want to kiss With / you

–   / Kissing you is fine

–   Kissing you and and holding you and putting my hand
        at the bottom of your back
        and and
        What?

–   It's the Putting, the Putting sounds

–   Putting

–   Something about it sounds

–   Putting? putting? putting. putting. putt ting. put ting I

–   No no no no, okay, no you're right, you're right,
        putting is fine, putting is Good, putting is – you're
        putting – putting – putting your hand at the bottom of
        my back

–   And and I'm kissing you

–   Yeah

–   I'm kissing you and and pressing you to me – can I say
        pressing?

– If I feel like I want to be pressed – which, now I think of it, yes, I do – then yes

– Good

– Really good

– Pressing you to me so Fucking Hard – is that

– Keep going

– That when you fall back into your own space the marks of me are all over you

– And me on you

– Like a a a a an imprint and a

– And me on you

– And I'm kissing your neck

– Marks of me are on you though

– I'm kissing, I'm kissing hard and I'm running my hands up and down your sides again and again and again and

– And I'm on you

– You're on me

– I'm on you

– And I want to feel you Shiver – shiver in a good way in a brilliant way

– Okay

– Yeah and and then, then I'm going to peel your dress off – slow – and and don't laugh

– Not laugh / ing

– / And you

– Not laughing but I'm also not a potato

– You can peel my clothes off

– You are also not a potato this is not potato / sex

– / And I'm I'm kissing you, all over

– Mmmm?

–   Yeah I'm kissing you all over and and I'm going to spread your legs

–   Oh?

–   Or you will spread them. When you are ready to spread them.

–   Mmmm

–   Uh huh

–   What was that

–   I don't know – so so

–   Or you could spread yours

–   Or. Yes. Or. I. Yes. I suppose I could spread mine.

–   Yes, why don't you spread yours?

–   Okay. Yes. Okay. I will spread my legs

–   Yeah?

–   Yeah

–   Yeah.

      Spread them.

–   But first. First. Could you spread yours?

–   No.

–   Alright. Alright.

      Spread them.

–   I. Um. I don't want to Spread them – could / we not say Spread

–   / You don't want / to spread them now

–   / sort of sounds like margarine or

–   Open?

–   Open.

      Yes. YES.

      Open. Open is good

–   Open

- So, so you open, we both open, but I open Your legs
- You open my / legs
- / Your legs and I want to Lick you, I want to extend my tongue and I want to lick you
- I'll lick you back
- .

  Okay.
- Yeah, I'll extend my tongue
- And my tongue is up inside you
- And I'll put my tongue up inside you
- And my fingers are up inside you now
- And I'll put my fingers up inside you
- And and – where? Where are / your fingers
- / Up inside your mouth, your arse, your
- Don't say arse
- Bum
- Don't say bum, I can't do
- Your Back Alley
- I have my hand up inside you

    She spits.
- Then I have my whole fist up inside you
- Ummmm
- You Like that
- I feel Conflicted about
- Then take your hand out
- I'm going to fuck you
- I'm going to fuck you straight back
- And I'm going to take my cock / and
- / AndI'mgoingtotakemyvaginaandputitOnyouFIRST

  .

–   What was that?

–   I get there first.

–   Yeah?

–   Yeah I am On you before you are In me

–   Are you

–   I'm going to take my vagina

–   Hang on

–   I'm taking my vagina

–   You can't Take your vagina

–   I am Taking My Vagina

–   You cannot Take a a a a a Gap

–   My Vagina is an Organ, my Vagina is not a Gap

–   It

–   How fucking Dare you – you are lucky to be anywhere
        Near my / Organ

–   / Your Organ is On My Organ

–   My Organ is On Your Organ

–   It's on my Big Hard Organ

–   It's All over it

–   Yeah, I'm pushing

–   I'm pushing back

–   And I'm pushing

–   And I'm Slamming it back down with my organ

–   And I'm

–   And I'm Enveloping you

–   Like. As in

–   I'm Surrounding you

–   Surround me, okay, yes, yes Surround me

–   I am Consuming you

–   Baby consume me

- And I – don't call me baby – I am Gorging on you, I am Making You My Dildo

- And so the the so / the

- / I am Drowning and Suffocating and Overwhelming you with my Giant Organ

- Well, it's cos / it's

- / I am Scissoring you

- That's

- I am Fucking Scissoring you to bits

- Is that

- I am Scissoring and Slicing you

- Then I am Screwing you

- And I am Spannering you

- I

- I am Completely Spannering you and I am Jumping you and Hiding you and
Chomping down upon you

- Not what I

- I am Blanketing and Locking you and Draining The Life of you with my Massive
Structured
Beautifully built
Almighty Vagina.

  .

  Alright?

  Are you Alright?

- .

- No?

- I just I

- No?

  Then I will Take Your Penis
  Sorry.

sorry.

– I. I. with the um. I. I feel. I.

– sorry I will take my Vagina. Off your penis.

Okay?

REVOLUTIONIZE THE WORLD. (DO NOT MARRY.)

– I don't understand why you're so – I just. I.

I wasn't expecting it.

.

It's not the. Sweetheart. It's not the uhhh. Sort of thing.
You Expect. Or look Out for.

Or.

Or.

Think About.

Ever.

We've never talked about it.

Ever.

Except at my Mum's uhhhh funeral Actually, and
because it wasn't

Because that wasn't a

Romantic – I didn't – a Romantic Setting, I'd sort of
maybe not really registered that as a a a a a Thing you
might be – I mean, I was trying to talk about Anything
so that I didn't have to think about her Dead Fucking
Body the other side of a a a curtain from us and our
conversation and those those Brown Shoes you were
wearing, those totally awful Brown shoes you'd Found
and put on and worn to my Mother's funeral as though
your sole objective that day was to make me Cry More
Not Less I'm sorry, I don't mean that – you're my
world my yadda yadda but the point is so I, I mean, we
could have been talking about about Anything or or or
or Any – so, so if that was you being Serious, if that was

you introducing that concept To our relationship at that point then I did not take that seriously and I'm sorry.

.

Except I'm Not fucking sorry because that was astonishingly poorly timed on your part.

.

I'm sorry. I am sorry for my language – I'm sorry about [that]

.

It was.

It was – I'm trying to find a

Words to.

.

What just happened was like

Was like.

It was like – what it was like was, was

Okay. So.

What I'm Feeling is.

What it was Like was if – Imagine if, okay – Imagine

If I just like, One Day

This is just – and this is just me Expressing how I'm feeling

Imagine if I one day – and this is it – if I one day

Waltzed in and was like. Like. Poppet. Sweetheart. Nightingale of mine and heart's desire. I love you. I love you to the edges of this earth and back, I love you body and heart and soul, I love you and I reckon to express this love, we should go and blow up the local Sainsbury's.

.

And then I Presented you
with a Massive Bomb
Upon a Vest.

On Bended Knee.

And Prior to this, okay, Prior to this moment, this
Bended Knee moment, let's imagine that the only
conversation we had ever had about Bombing or
or or Suicide Bombers in any sense, was, in fact, a
sort of vague chat in which maybe one of us might
have expressed slightly hesitant but not entirely
unpredictable – given our bleeding-heart liberalism –
empathy towards said suicide bombers who had lost
everything in a war that you and I from our privileged
position understand very little about in any real sense at
least – and I'm proud of that empathy, that empathy is
a Good Thing – but Imagine though, imagine, that that
slightly vague experience had been, in fact, the only
conversation we had Ever had about bombing and then
in I stroll with a suicide vest and suggest that we go
and blow up the local supermarket in the sort of tone
that suggested that that had been the plan all along – I
mean, imagine your surprise.

Imagine

your surprise.

–   I didn't Suggest that we blow up a supermarket /
       together

–   / Of course you didn't – that was a fu – that was a
       Metaphor, that was a

       I wish you had.

–   We've been to weddings together

–   We have watched suicide bomb reports on the news
       together but that doesn't

–   I just told you I loved you

–   No you didn't

- I just told you I loved you
- Nope
- And that I wanted to spend the rest of my life with you
- Presenting me with an enormous diamond. Or bomb. Does not mean those things.
- You Love diamonds.
- I feel Concerned

About where diamonds come from.

    .

- I just want you to be my wife, it's not a.

It wasn't a.

I didn't Find those shoes – I Bought those shoes specifically for –

    .

We can get a Different ring.

I want to have a life with you – I just said I want to have a life with you

- No you didn't
- All I said was I wanted to live my life Next to yours
- No you didn't
- That I wanted to love you forever
- That isn't what you said
- I just said that I just wanted to commit to you
- Nnnno
- I said that you're The most important human being to me
- No
- That you're a really important person in my life
- Not what you said
- That you're a person in my life
- Nope

–   That you make me smile every time I see you

–   No

–   That you you make me laugh more than anyone

–   No

–   That I want to to buy Dogs and then bury those dogs in a back garden we share

–   No

–   I said I wanted to do my online food shop with you and go on all my main holidays with you and and

–   Did not hear you say a single one of those words

–   That I want to bring up small humans that we sort of might make together

–   No

–   That I want to share values and dinners and and baths with you

–   No

–   That I want I want

         What I said was. I wanted. Security. With you.

–   Those words didn't come out of your mouth

         .

–   I just said

–   No

–   All I Said was

–   Nah

–   It.

–   No you didn't

–   I'm. I want. It's. I.

         .

–   You Essentially said you wanted to reduce your income tax.

–   .

What?

- And inherit my pension.

- I did not

- That you can decide what to do with my body if I happen to die in another country

- Those words did not – another what / now

- That you want me to give up my name

- You can you can / Keep your

- / That you want to turn me into Chattel

- If – I just

- A thing to be traded

- Can we

- That I am to become your possession, your property, a thing you own – given to you by a man I don't really speak to anymore holding a bunch of fucking bluebells and wearing a meringue in some kind of enormous shaming event in which I am supposed to be a Silent Walking Symbol of virginity yet simultaneously be Totally Relaxed about all the sex we are having whilst you get to walk around Doing All The Talking in a suit

- It doesn't Mean those things anymore

- What does it mean then?

    .

- I want to marry you.

    I want you to be my wife.

    My partner.

    .

- I am not entirely sure I believe in those things.

- Is this.

    Are you.

    I want to marry

    I want to

I want

I.

Is. Is this. is this just occurring to you Now?

– No.

Yes.

Maybe.

I don't know.

REVOLUTIONIZE THE WORK. (ENGAGE WITH IT.)

– I um. I don't. Sorry. No. I don't understand.

– That's fine

– No, it's not fine.

– I feel very fine about it.

– Yes, You feel – You feel fine. I do not feel fine about it.

.

– I don't want to work Mondays.

That feels fairly straightforward.

– Okay. And can you tell me Why you don't want to work Mondays?

– I want to get more sleep

– On Mondays?

– I want to sleep more

– We all want to sleep more

– Then maybe we should all do something about that.

.

I want to walk my dogs more. I have inherited a house in the countryside that has a path that goes from my doorstep and leads through the garden that is just potatoes and then bluebells – when it is the right time for bluebells – and that path then leads to fields and keeps going through fields and past a brook and those fields, they back onto a little wood where there are larks and nightingales and I want to walk in that wood. With my dogs. On a Monday.

It's very beautiful.

– I know it is. I know it is, you've had me and my girlfriend over for dinner, it's very fucking beautiful, it felt very fucking beautiful as we stood in your potato patch, I don't – .

.

I'm sorry.

.

– I don't want to do that anymore. I don't want to cook for hours. I don't want to have people over for dinner anymore because I want to Sleep more and I want to walk my dogs more often in the woods.

.

– We've put vending machines in the corridors.

– I don't care.

– We've put vending machines in and we're building a gym in the basement.

– I don't want those things.

– You're being very obtuse.

– I'm being very clear.

.

– Are you pregnant?

– Do I Look pregnant?

– .

I'd believe you if you said you were. You don't look Not pregnant.

– I'm not pregnant.

– Are you Trying to get pregnant?

– That's not really any of your business

–   It Is if I need to recruit someone else

–   I'm not trying to get pregnant

        .

–   Do you Want to Try to get pregnant

–   What I want to try to do is not your – no. No, I don't
        want to do that

–   Women want that – it's okay

–   I don't want that

–   You're a real career girl?

–   I just want more sleep

–   Do you want to do a course? Is that it? Do you want to
        further your studies?

–   Not really.

–   Ah. Okay. Okay. You're not where you thought you
        Might be

–   No, I'm not, but that's not the

–   Where you thought you Could be

–   That's not

–   In fact, because – and this is, this is really – I'm the First
        person in my family to go to university, okay. And now
        look. A course might help you tap into whatever it is
        you

–   I'm the first person in my family to keep all their fingers
        past the age of twenty-one.

        .

–   We really appreciate your labour.

–   I'm fine.

–   You don't Seem fine

–   I'm really fine

–   It's okay that you're Not fine

–   I am fine.

–   It's okay. We're talking about some intense things. We can use one of the Relax rooms

–   I'm fine.

–   You really care about this

–   I don't care. I'm just being clear with you.

–   You Sound a little bit like you care.

–   I

–   And we can help with that. Perhaps you should look at doing a course.

–   I just want more time off

–   Mondays off

–   Mondays off. Initially.

.

–   Are you Ill?

–   No

–   Okay, is it cancer?

–   No

–   Is it terminal? Is it piles, do you have haemorrhoids?

–   Not at the minute

–   That's disgusting

–   I just want to work less. Don't you?

–   Are you having a Mental Fucking Breakdown?

.

I'm sorry. I apologise for my language.

The vending machines have chocolate and fizzy drinks and sandwiches and flavoured water in them.

–   I don't care about those things.

–   What if you could bring your dogs into the work environment? Would that make things better? Would you feel better about working Mondays then?

\-   I want to walk my dogs through things that grow in the woods.

\-   There are trees near here. You could walk your dogs, your – what kind of dogs

\-   Pitbulls.

          .

\-   Are you

\-   Deadly.

          .

\-   You could walk your Pitbulls by the trees near here in your lunchbreak and get a sandwich from the vending machine and you could watch them Piss all over the grass and then you could go to the gym after your shift and read one of the complimentary magazines after your cool down

\-   I don't think you're listening.

\-   We've put a bar on the rooftop terrace and we're doing Happy Hour Fridays. We could do Happy Hour Mondays as well, would that help? There are beers and wines and the spritzers and the Cosmopolitans are very popular with the girls, we can bring Happy Hour in on a Monday as well, if you like, and we could relax the No Dogs and the No Smoking rules because we want it to be fun, we want it to be a genuinely fun working environment

\-   It's work. It's not a real bar.

\-   It's the work bar.

\-   That doesn't make any sense

\-   What dyou – of course it – it's the work bar.

\-   Just because you charge your employees for a beer in the same building in which they work and then encourage them to return to their jobs does not make it a Real Thing – I won't work on Mondays anymore.

\-   Do you want a swimming pool – is that it?

–   No.

–   Because you can – you can have it all

–   I don't know what that means

–   All of it. You can have everything

    We can organise Spa days. Spa days can be on
    Wednesdays and we'll do more face masks and more
    pampering and we'll get faster, tougher, bigger fucking
    treadmills to make your body tighter and make your
    body softer and we'll have More chocolate and More
    wine and we'll have more fun and be more focused
    than you've ever been. Right here. Okay.

–   No. Thank you.

–   Would you like a work handbag?

–   No.

–   They can cost £2000, we can make that an option, we
    can make that part of your pay packet

–   No. Thank you.

–   Do you want a pay rise? Is that it? Do you want to be
    paid as much as

    as the

    *Perhaps it's not clear whether the actor has forgotten their line,
    or it is the character tripping over a word.*

    as the

    the – sorry – as the boys?

    .

    Stop smiling.

–   *(Again, is this character or actor?)* I'm Contracted to smile

–   Not in meetings, you aren't Contracted to smile in
    meetings – Stop Smiling

–   You stop smiling.

–   I'm serious. Stop Smiling.

–   This is just my face – I Want to smile at the moment,
    you can't tell me what to do with my face

–   Whilst you're in here I Own your face

–   No you don't

–   Yes I do

–   No you don't own my face

–   I do

It feels like the actors aren't sticking to the lines, perhaps.

.

Okay fine I don't Own your face but I do Object to, I don't like you smiling like that whilst you're being so obtuse, I'm saying that you can bring your dogs into the work bar

–   And I'm saying I refuse to recognise that as a real or legitimate space

–   You Signed the petition Asking for the vending machines

–   I don't want to work on Mondays

–   You Signed it

–   Then that was a mistake. And I apologise.

–   I don't accept your apology

–   That is your right

–   The Problem is – and this is the Problem – the Problem is is that I don't understand

–   I want Mondays off.

–   Do you feel you'll be more productive?

–   That's not my motivation.

–   Is it about protest?

–   It's about sleep.

–   Because you've already got so much – is the thing – you already have so much

–   It's just one day.

–   Let me pour you a a a a a drink

–   I don't want a drink

–   Have a chocolate bar

–   I don't want a chocolate bar

–   Everyone Wants a ch ch ch – ch.

    a Chocolate bar

–   I don't.

–   But it makes women happy.

–   I'll see you on Tuesday.

–   .

REVOLUTIONIZE THE BODY (MAKE IT SEXUALLY AVAILABLE. CONSTANTLY).

There are at least three people in this scene.

–   I don't understand

–   I'm not sure either of us Fully understands

–   No

–   It's – we'd really like to

–   We'd absolutely like to

–   I'd Love to understand – I'd Love to know where your head is at, what your your Thought process was

–   What led you

–   Absolutely, what Led you

–   Or – or, if I can just butt / in

–   / Please / do

–   / Perhaps Who led you, even, if I could be so so Bold

–   Quite

–   Because if Someone Else has led you

–   Well then that would be Concerning

–   Indeed

–   That would suggest

- Suggest
- That this was part of a wider problem as opposed to
- As opposed to
- A One Off.
- Because it's been a shock
- A Big shock
- For all of us
- We've never – sorry – I am so sorry – I am Talking For you
- You are
- I'm just Talking For you without checking in with
- It's fine
- Would you listen to me Talking For You – isn't that hilarious
- I feel fine about
- Because I think I Can say for both of us
- Absolutely
- When I say that we have never seen anything like it
- No
- Never
- Not once
- And – and I'm going to speak for you again
- I'm entirely happy for you to do so – we're a / team
- / A team, we are – I've interrupted you though, interrupting isn't very
- It's fine
- Team-like, but I suppose my point is
- Our point is
- Precisely, Our Point is what the Fuck you thought you were doing.

.

-     Or.

-     Not or. Not really Or, there isn't really an Or

-     Well

-     No Or about it

-     I suppose not

-     Because I think we'd all really like to know – myself and yourself

-     Yes

-     And the entire team really, not to mention our customers

-     Yes – the Customers, the Customers are who I'm really concerned about

-     Well, quite

-     Because we're getting complaints

-     Hundreds of complaints

-     Tens of complaints

-     Several complaints

-     And the reaction

-     On on Social media

-     Yes

-     On social media has already been Flooding in

-     Storming in

-     And the response really, from all corners has been:

  What the Fuck did she think she was doing – has anyone offered you a glass of water?

-     .

  No.

-     That's terribly rude

-     of us – I apologise

-     Because I am aware – Fully aware

-     Completely aware

—   Aware – do you know what I'm going to say

—   well

—   One Mind – we're like One Mind

—   We're a team

—   The Engine Room

—   We're Aware, okay

—   Very Aware

—   We're So Aware

—   That

—   That

—   You're our customer too

—   One mind.

—   And it's really important – really crucially important – that We Understand our customers

—   Essential

—   It's how the company operates

—   It's on our branding

—   It's in our fucking logo – I have to apologise for my language – I do

—   It's because we feel strongly

—   We feel very passionate

—   We do

—   So – again – we'd really, really, really love to know

—   What the fuck you thought you were doing

—   What the fuck you thought you were doing lying in the middle of Aisle Seven with your dress over your head.

.

—   You will have to pay for those melons.

We literally cannot resell those melons.

—   And we want you to Have those melons

- Of course

- The point is, we're Happy you chose our store as the place in which you wish to Buy those melons

- We fly those melons in from all sorts of countries so that you can just Have them

- Without having to think about where they came from

- That's a thing we're really proud of

- That's a choice we're really happy you can freely make

- We made the label 'these watermelons come from Florida via Guatemala and back' really very small indeed, just so that you don't have to feel guilty

- Guilt-free shopping is particularly important to us

- We want you to have it all and not feel guilty

- Because you Absolutely can

- But we're Concerned about

- Yes what we're really concerned about is

- Why you chose our supermarket as the place in which to lie down and expose yourself

- There is Watermelon All Over Aisle Seven

- Which is Hazardous

- Which puts Our customers at risk

- Do you see?

- And your choice to lie down and reveal your body

- Your Breasts were fully on show

- That Choice that You made to Lie down

- Not to mention your stomach and your ribs

- That choice that you made had an impact on our Other patrons in that moment

- Because no one Asked to see that

- No one Wanted to see your flesh in Aisle Seven

- People go to Aisle Seven to buy their dairy products

–   To select their yoghurts and their milk, their cheese and
      their cream

–   Not to see your folds of skin

–   And Certainly not to see your hand upon your knickers

–   Or your little sausage legs wide open surrounded by
      cereal boxes and potatoes

–   Or you Pulling your knickers down, in fact

–   Or your flab. Quite frankly. Your curdled flab.
      The physical evidence of your regret at consuming
      presumably an entire Wheel of Cheese every night
      since you were eleven was not what our unwitting
      shoppers had selected to see when they rolled into
      Aisle Seven to select their fat free cottage cheese.

–   So you see

–   No one wanted to see your bingo wings

–   What we're dying to know

–   Or your muffin top

–   What we

–   Or your pork belly

–   So

      *(Perhaps it's not clear whether the actors have forgotten their
      lines at this point, or it is the characters tripping over a word.)*
      So. So Um to

–   Or your fucking chicken thighs you fucking chicken
      thighs your horrible fucking chicken thighs – I

      I

–   Don't laugh

–   Not laughing not laughing.

      .

      I apologise.

      .

–   I have felt very
      tired lately.

74

I could fall asleep standing straight up.

I'm sorry about the watermelon.

I'm not sorry about the watermelon.

.

Where my body stops and the air around it starts
has felt a little like this long continuous line of a
battleground for about my whole life, I think.

Fortify.

.

I have cut my eyelashes off. I have covered myself
in coal and mud. I have bandaged my body up and
made myself a collection of straight edges. Fortify. I
have rubbed iodine, bleach and the gut of a rabbit into
my skin until it began to burn. I have nearly emptied
my body of its organs. I stopped eating for one year
and three days, my body a bouquet of shell bone. I
have eaten only animal fat until I rolled, bubbled and
whaled and came quite close to popping. Fortify. Make
my edges clear. Where I begin and air stops is my
motherland. No? I have sat under sun lamps until my
skin crackled, spat and blistered. I have pulled my hair
out with my fingers and my teeth out with pliers. I have
wrapped myself in clingfilm, foil, clothes, make-up and
barbed wire.

No fortification strong enough.

Nothing to stop them wanting to come in.

Lie down.

Lie down and become available. Constantly. Want to
be entered. Constantly. It cannot be an Invasion, if you
want it. They Cannot Invade if you Want It. Open your
legs and throw your dress over your head, pull your
knickers down and want it and they can invade you no
longer.

Get wet.

Get wet.

Get wetter.

Turn on. Turn on. Turn on.

And want it. And want it. Constantly. Constantly.
Constantly want it. Remove the edges of your body.
Choose. My body is no battleground, there is no longer
a line of defense – I Am Open. There are borders
here no more. This body this land is unattackable,
unprotected, unconquerable, unclaimable, no different
from air around it or bodies coming in because there Is
no in to come into, you cannot overpower it because I
have given it you cannot rape it because I choose it you
cannot take because I give it and because I choose it I
choose it I choose it

Constantly.

This World Can Never Attack Me Again.

Because I Choose it. Over and Again and Again and
Over.

.

– I.

– *(Is this the character or the actor?)* I'm sorry. I'm not sure
what happens now?

– .

Act Two.

REVOLUTIONIZE THE WORLD (DON'T REPRODUCE).

This Act is continuous. The titles do not break the action.

A farm. DINAH holds AGNES's hand. It doesn't matter if GRANDMA looks very young.

DINAH: I don't sleep anymore.

Do you?

.

Hello.

I wanted to tell you that I understood. That I had reached a place of total acceptance that I had developed the kind of understanding that rooted deep, deep enough to not care about what the outcome of this conversation might be.

But of course that isn't the case.

.

Do I look at all different then?

.

GRANDMA: You're a little taller probably.

I don't have much skill for remembering faces.

DINAH: Nothing about my eyes or my smile?

GRANDMA: Haven't seen you smile. Couldn't comment.

DINAH: I'm finding it hard to.

It's like smog. Or water. It's not as light as it used to be – Air, I'm talking about the Air, I.

It's physically impossible. Sleeping.

I'm beyond feeling it now.

.

The plan was to get in the car and drive for
three days – which we did – to bring you bread
and jam – which we did – to pick you flowers –
which we did – and to stand in front of you and
tell you that I understand. That I completely
understand. And that I forgive you. And then
we would drive home but we would stop at the
end of the first day, not Drive continuously as
we did on our way here, but stop and pull in
somewhere by a little wood and sleep.

.

But I don't understand.

And this morning, there was a line across the
sky, a completely legible black line that seemed
to mark the journey back, away from you
and the temptation to take that was enormous
because I know you probably won't help
me you probably don't give a and there is
something about all of this that I can Bear I can
shoulder I can do, but Agnes – Agnes's mouth
bleeds, she scratches and she scratches at it until
it bleeds and she has started to stop talking, she
won't eat, she won't lift her hands, she can't
keep hold of a thing, not a thing, she is starting
to disappear entirely and and and I think if you
can tell her she came from somewhere good
then it might stop.

.

GRANDMA: Agnes?

DINAH: .

This is Agnes.

She gave you the bluebells

GRANDMA: She dropped the bluebells

DINAH: She's tired. She can't hold any – she's tired.

GRANDMA: Everybody's tired all of a sudden

DINAH: *(Is this the actor or the character?)* This is Hard – this is really getting Harder I

I feel. I'm. Sorry.

Okay.

.

This looks wonderful. Really. Really. Is it all home grown?

GRANDMA: I grew it. If that's what you mean. Or I killed it. If that's what you mean.

DINAH: It's so impressive.

What an achievement.

It's really remarkable, it's.

.

This is Agnes. Your Granddaughter. Agnes.

GRANDMA: .

Shall we eat.

DINAH: Your granddaughter. Agnes.

GRANDMA: That'll be impossible, Dinah.

DINAH: Your granddaughter. Agnes.

GRANDMA: I have no granddaughter.

DINAH: Your flesh and blood. Your granddaughter. Agnes.

GRANDMA: My flesh and my blood are all contained within my body.

DINAH: Agnes was born of my body, I was born of your body.

GRANDMA: You're your own body.

DINAH: I don't understand, I'm your child

GRANDMA: I have no children.

I had no children.

REVOLUTIONIZE THE WORK (DON'T DO IT).

Serve the potatoes then Agnes.

AGNES: looks.

DINAH: I

GRANDMA: There's butter over there, and there's wine on that shelf.

Pour it.

DINAH: She doesn't

GRANDMA: She can pour some wine. Her hands aren't bleeding. She has all her fingers.

DINAH: She's your granddaughter.

GRANDMA: There's meat. She can carve it.

DINAH: This is the first time I have sat with my family around me and

GRANDMA: I'm not your family, Dinah.

.

DINAH: Will we say Grace?

GRANDMA: Cut some of that bread.

DINAH: We should say Grace

GRANDMA: Can say what the fuck you like.

DINAH: We always used to say Grace

GRANDMA: Put salt on the potatoes.

DINAH: Such Excitement when it was My turn to say Grace

GRANDMA: You can get that cheese from the side there.

DINAH: Sitting at the Big table giving thanks for watermelons – I Always gave thanks for watermelons

GRANDMA: You. Say Grace then /

/ AGNES sings. It hurts. She stops.

REVOLUTIONIZE THE LANGUAGE
(THAT WORD DOESN'T EXIST HERE).

GRANDMA: I said Grace. That wasn't Grace.

AGNES: Grayce. Grayssss. Grace. ssssss. I

DINAH: It was beautiful, it was like a

AGNES::   Buuuuuutifull I don't

DINAH: Little nightingale, it was lovely and and perfect and

AGNES: Luv luvvvv luvl I I'm sorry I don't [understand]

DINAH: She

GRANDMA: I said Grace not

DINAH: Be kind. Be kind, please. Be kind.

AGNES: Kynd. Kiiiind. Kind. Kind. I don't. I'm sorry. I don't understand. I. I. *(Is this the actor's confusion, or the character?)* I'm sorry, I really don't understand.

DINAH: You don't have to under[stand] – she doesn't have to [understand] – it gets harder and harder and

REVOLUTIONIZE THE WORLD
(DON'T ASSOCIATE WITH MEN)

A man enters.

GRANDMA: Get out

The man leaves.

REVOLUTIONIZE THE BODY (STOP EATING).

GRANDMA: Will she not eat?

DINAH: Please don't ask that.

REVOLUTIONIZE THE BODY / THE LANGUAGE (STOP SPEAKING).

GRANDMA: Do you want something?

AGNES: .

GRANDMA: What does she want?

AGNES smiles.

REVOLUTIONIZE THE BODY (START TO SHUT IT DOWN).

GRANDMA: Her mouth is bleeding.

DINAH: You got trapped. You were completely trapped. Daddy beat you up. He kicked the living shit out of you.

My Daddy – that man you lived with and had sex with and children were then produced – He used to Jump. With Boots on.

Upon your neck.

He used to hold a lit match between your legs and if you flinched he would punch upwards, breaking the walls of your cunt.

He used to bite your breasts until they bled. He used to kick your knees for hours, not particularly hard, not his hardest, but kick until his back was drenched in sweat and your bones were shattered.

He used to rape you, he used to –

(Is this the character or the actor?) Sorry – sorry – am I Sexualising all this a bit too um. Am I making this Sexy – he used to, okay, okay okay okay okay, my Daddy used to beat the crap out of you and you had to get out, you had to get out and forget you had children, forget it all and begin again, I can understand that

AGNES retches.

GRANDMA: Not what happened.

            That didn't happen, none of that happened.

DINAH: My father was the kindest man – I'm trying to
            – so you felt you'd gotten very ill. You'd fallen
            very terribly gravely ill – can I smoke

GRANDMA: Can do what the fuck you like

DINAH: You were diseased, riddled with it, getting
            weaker by the day and you had to retreat you
            had to go away rather than know your family
            had to watch you suffer, forget it all, forget it
            all forget all the children and begin again, I can
            understand that. Though of course you should
            be dead.

GRANDMA: Never been ill a day in my life.

DINAH: You were depressed. Contemplating suicide.
            It was too awful to imagine that And have
            children.

GRANDMA: Not so.

            AGNES vomits.

DINAH: *(Is this the character or the actor??)* That is
            Disgusting – I am just Trying – trying to get an
            insight into, some understanding of, because it
            seems I came from nowhere kind, nowhere kind
            and I haven't been able to give anything good
            to my girl, not one good thing and now – was it
            the environment – did you feel a sudden jolt, a
            sudden panic that you had offloaded such a Dent
            into the world, a whole new carbon footprint, a
            new person to help deplete the fish stocks and
            pollute the skies and get on planes on planes on
            planes and contribute to the rise of the sea, was
            that why you left me on my fourth birthday and
            decided to renounce your children – more than
            that – deny you'd ever birthed them in the first
            place – the others are all Dead by the way so my
            breathing, my being here feels miraculous – did
            you do it for love of the planet

GRANDMA: No

DINAH: For the love of a man

GRANDMA: No

DINAH: For the love of a woman

GRANDMA: No

DINAH: Say you did for the love of something, for one good thing, one good reason, she's splitting into the smallest pieces, she has never known goodness

GRANDMA: There isn't much goodness.

DINAH: Was it that I waged a little war upon your body?

Was it that I ruined smooth lines – was it that everyone says it's the most natural thing a woman Can possibly do but it's havoc and perhaps I shattered your hips in the process and shit is everywhere, suddenly shit is everywhere, was it that?

Was it because I was a girl?

If I had had a dick you could have chopped it off in protest, I could have been political – was it that?

Did I break your heart?

Did I ruin your life?

Did I make you incapable of love – did you hold a thing so big and so fucking precious near your ribs and then in I came and destroyed it, in I came – or out I came – splitting your body in two and someone put me up at your breast up near your heart and where there had been promise and love and hope there was fucking pus?

Tell her.

Tell her.

Tell her so she can know goodness. Tell me so I
can sleep – *(Is this the character or the actor??!)* I
am so so very tired I don't know what to do.

.

*GRANDMA and AGNES pick up their knives and forks. They
chop their tongues out.*

Act Three

GALVANISE

The line between actor and character can be paper thin here. At some point, the actors will have to be in more than one scene at the same time. It is okay to find that difficult.

– OH MY GOD I'VE ABSOLUTELY FUCKING CRACKED IT.

.

– I am never aroused by porn. I am never aroused by porn. I am never aroused by porn. Porn. Never. Arouses me.

– I REFUSE TO BAKE THE FOLLOWING

– Naaaaaaailed it!

.

Sorry.

.

THE FOLLOWING ITEMS. I REFUSE TO BAKE CUPCAKES. I PARTICULARLY REFUSE TO BAKE HEART-SHAPED GOODS. I DO NOT SELL GLITTER.

Please click on About Me for more info

– I Will close my eyes if I see a pornographic

and feedback.

picture and yes, I will be
compiling a petition. In
Relation. To it.
And a survey. And yes,
yes, I probably will run
for parliament.
Thank you.
Thank you so much.

–   Does this pass the
Bechdel test?

–   No. No, I don't
think so.

–   Hymens! Unruptured
hymens for sale.
Perfectly intact.
Hymens! Come and
buy our hymens –
carefully removed,
perfectly intact,
utterly unravished!

–   Because. Okay. Because. And this is exciting, this is
really the Nuts but –
Shit.

Leaves.

–   What're you doing?

–   *(Is this the actor or the character?)* Ummmm.

–   What're you Doing?

–   None of your beeswax

–   Think it is my beeswax

–   Just cos you're wearing A Uniform does not mean it is
your beeswax.

–   That is Exactly what it means

You know you're not supposed to be down here.

–   Who says?

–   Law.

–   This alley backs onto my house

–   Right

–   Not that it Is any of your beeswax, but this alley backs onto my property.

–   Still can't be down here

–   Why not?

–   For your own safety. Not allowed in alleys.
You know that.

–   WE'VE GOT LITERALLY SO MUCH WORK TO DO!

–   She is Fiercely intelligent. She can be a little bit emotional, agreed, but she is fiercely intelligent – a little on the aggressive side. But she's fearless too. Fearless. And occasionally manipulative. She's a really vital member of the team. She's adjectives. And. *(Perhaps it's not clear whether the actor has forgotten their line, or it is the character tripping over a word.)* She's lots of adjectives and describing words.

Him? He's great.

–   Because. Okay.
Because. And this is
exciting. It is it is it is.
Just need a second to.
Catch my.
But I've been
thinking. I've been
taking Time and Space

to Think very deeply
and I've got this feeling
all the way down to my
bones, to my marrow,
that that okay, that –
and this is fucking It   –   I'm not really sure I get
your point.

That.   .
Um. That.   –   He seems very
thinking   Unhappy
that.   –   That's not unusual
                       –   He cries. All of the time.
                       –   He's a child.
                       –   He drew this picture
                              yesterday.
                       –   Okay.

–   I HAVE GOT   Alright.
       LITERALLY NO   You want me to hang
       MAKE-UP ON   it on my fridge?

                       –   That's not my – I'm just
                              trying to figure out if
                              there are things Going
                              On at home that might
                              explain some of his
                              feelings.

                       –   His feelings?

                       –   He said this picture was
                              called 'Me and My
                              Cellulite'

                       –   Okay.

                       –   We talked about wishes
                              yesterday. He said he
                              wished he had a thigh
                              gap.

                              .

–   I have been thinking.   –   Right?

–   He had one piece of
watermelon in his
lunchbox today.

He says he's fat. He
says he's disgustingly
fat.

–   Scuse me?   –   He is. Isn't he?
Ummm   They're all fat.
                       Aren't they?
You're supposed to   –   He's four.
OI. OI. OI   –   Okay – What're you
                       Doing?

                       .

–   Me?

–   Yeah you – What're you Doing?

–   I'm making T-shirts. And pants. And pencil cases.
Merch.

–   Merch?

–   Merchandise.

–   What d'you   –   I HAVE BEEN
                             THINKING.

     .

–   This one says NO SEXISM

–   You cannot be

–   This one says STOP BEING SEXIST. Merch.

–   You have to be kidding

–   This one says LET'S BE EQUAL YEAH?

     .

She chops her head off.

– takes a big breath, ready to speak –

–   Who is that man? Mowing the lawn? His feet are
bleeding.

\-   Ummmmmm. Sorry. Hang on a. I'm not supposed to
    do this one – it's

\-   Who is that man? Mowing the lawn? His feet are
    bleeding.

\-   No, I'm not in

\-   No – seriously. Who is that man? Mowing the lawn?
    His feet are bleeding.

\-   Ohhh. Him? He raped
    that girl. The
    disabled one.
    He's doing community   –   Hymens! Still for sale!
    service   Reduced! Hymens,
                                    come and get your
                                    hymens!

\-   Adverb adjective noun. Adverb adjective noun. Adverb
    adjective noun. Do you see?

\-   The thing is – the Thing that I've been thinking

\-   Yeah I absolutely wholeheartedly Get that, I really Do,
    it's just that it's near impossible with no evidence, dyou
    know what I mean?

\-   I

\-   Yeah, d'you know what I mean?

\-   I'm sorry, I literally have no idea what you

    With the fact of the matter of me being a police officer
    that you have called here to the scene of the crime

\-   Oh. Yes. Right. Um. Evidence. You said something
    about

    Evidence

\-   Yes exactly, in that there is none so it's impossible to
    push on in our investigations at the time being for now
    unfortunately

\-   With the –

Okay.   –   Sorry to interrupt
Hang on a, because it's
getting impossible to Think.
I haven't got any stuff.

–   Yeah no sure, absolutely, but that could of course
just be a Choice you've made in terms of your living
arrangements – you would need to prove that you Had
stuff

–   I'm really tired

–   Sure   –   Sorry, but

–   Um, the uh, my windows are all smashed

–   Yeah, but again, who's to say
You didn't do that yourself

–   I've got blood all over my legs

–   I'm not judging   –   Sorry to

–   My blood is everywhere

–   Yeah, but it's just that
there's no evidence

                       –   Sorry to interrupt

–   Yeah?

–   I just I wanted to

–   You're fine

–   I just – I wanted to just ask if you could not do that

–   Do what

–   That thing you're about to do – be fucked in your
arsehole by that dog whilst those men jizz on your face
til you vomit and they make you eat it up again – could
you not do that?

     .

–   Ummm. It's sort of the
Main Action of the scene.

–   Totally appreciate
that – really do. Bills   –   Um.

to pay and and that.
It's just that everyone
thinks that's sex now.

–   Would I describe
    myself as a [feminist] –
    yeah Absolutely,
    Absolutely. I mean, as
    a Father of a girl –
    how could I not be?

–   Would I describe
    myself [as a feminist] –
    of course, of course –
    I'm married. To A
    Woman. How could
    I not be? Please!

–   Would I – I've got
    a mother haven't I?
    Think About That.

–   Naturally. I walk past
    women all the time.
    Course I am.

–   I've seen a woman
    before. Round things.
    Absolutely I support
    the round ones. 100%.

–   I'd need to See a
    woman I think before
    I said if I was one for
    sure, I'd need to know
    what it was exactly I
    was supporting, but
    essentially, yeah, sure

–   Yes. I'm a Human, so.
    Yes.

–   Can't feel my legs.

–   *(Throws a bucket of water
    over herself and slaps
    herself.)*
    THIS FEELS
    AMAZING
    GENUINELY
    INCREDIBLE. I

    AM HAVING A
    WONDERFUL TIME.

–   I think I thought it was –   THIS FEELS
something else.   AMAZING
SHUT THE FUCK UP.

I think. I think I thought it was something smaller than
it is. And actually. Actually it's Enormous. Actually
it's a Massive Fuck Off Explosion we're after. Because
really. Really there's nowhere else to go.

                              –   An Englishman,
                                   Irishman and a
                                   Scottishman all go into a
                                   bar
                              –   Yeah
                              –   RAPE!

There is a human in   *They laugh.*
between the two people   –   That is undoubtedly
speaking.   funny

–   I'm so sorry

–   Are you okay?

–   No, I'm so sorry – I feel awful, but

–   What is it?

–   It's just that. Well.

     You're trespassing.

–   Sorry?

–   On my property – you're trespassing – just. Here. See.
     Trespass – you're um. You're trespassing.

     .

–   Oh God, am I really?

–   Mmmm   –   Adverb adjective noun.

–   I had no / idea   Adverb
                                   adjective noun.

– / Yeah, no, it's – you're   Adverb adjective noun.
   / trespassing

– / God, how embarrassing /

– / No, it's fine, it's just –
   belongs to me / so

– / I feel Awful / Totally

– / These things happen,
   it's just, you know / it

– / Absolutely – I feel /
   terrible

– No it's – not to worry.

   Need to get You a bigger
   No Trespassing sign.

   They laugh.

– *(Running round.)* My choice my choice

my choice my choice	–	Dearly beloved
my choice my choice	–	No
my choice my choice	–	We are gathered here
my choice my choice		today
my choice my choice	–	Absolutely fucking not
my choice my choice	–	In the Sight of
choice my choice my	–	No way Jose
choice my choice my	–	Please.
choice my choice my	–	No
choice my choice my	–	Please?
choice my choice my	–	No
choice my choice my	–	Go On
choice my choice my	–	I'm not marrying him
choice my choice my	–	Give it a go
choice my choice my	–	He raped me.
choice my choice my	–	Yeah but
choice my choice my	–	And I'm twelve
choice my choice my	–	But this is nicest for
choice my choice my		everyone
choice my choice my		

choice my choice my
choice my choice my
choice my choice my
choice my choice my
choice my choice my
choice my choice my
choice – it really Is Better
and safest and Nicest
for everyone

Yes, see Nicest for
everyone

if You stay Indoors
because otherwise
you might get attacked
and we can all go
Outdoors but because   –
none of You will be
Outdoors then none of
Us will be able to attack
you so that's Nicest

WOMAN FOR SALE!
WHOLE HUMAN
FOR SALE! IN THE
NAME OF AHM
SOMETHING
REALLY BIG –
WOMAN FOR SALE,
ENTIRE WOMAN
FOR SALE

–   Still trespassing

–   Oops!

They laugh.

It's because it's So Easy –
So Easy to do   –

I'm not doing it
But I'm needed over
there

–   Hymens are for sale,   –
just at the back there by –
the watermelons and
the bluebells and the
potatoes and the cup-
cakes and some canned
goods.

I'm tired
He's mowing the lawn
because he raped
someone
This is called Me
and My Cellulite
Why had everyone in
her family lost

–   YOU CAN'T   Adjective adverb noun.
    TRESPASS HERE   Adjective adverb
    I AM HOLDING   noun. And so on.
    A FUCKING NO
    TRESPASS SIGN
    FOR A REASON   My choice my choice
    YOU ABSOLUTE   my choice
    FUCKTARD.   .

                       Absolutely.

–   Brilliant

                   –   Isn't it? I am having
                       THE BEST TIME

–   Not possible because
    I am / HAVING THE
    BEST TIME

–   / THE BEST TIME

–   Could you shut up?

–   Porn is not arousing –   –   My choice my choice
    porn never ever   my choice
    ever arousing
                                .

–   Except when it is horse   And then you're
                                supposed to say...

    porn.   .
    Obviously.

– Well. Obviously.   – And then it's   – Aren't you a
   Obviously when   your line.   bit exhausted?
   it is horse porn   I Say. My choice   Hasn't the blood
   then that is a   my choice my   drained from
   different matter.   choice...   you?
   Obviously that   And then you   .
   is entirely   say...
   arousing.   .   Don't you feel a
                                            little like

97

–   Dolphins rape other dolphins of course.
–   Of course
–   It happens in the natural world all the time which is probably why humans do it – because nature does it first and I don't think it's that we're anthropo-morphising their behaviour to justify our behaviour – I don't think it's that at all
–   No not at all – do you know your lines?
–   No, not a single one I've been making the whole thing up

My choice my choice my choice.

.

Hymens

.

Aaaaand Fat little boys and stuff.

And merchandise and alleys and threesomes and make-up and stuff and and and and and and so on and so forth and so on and adjectives and describing words and more describing words and then some more describing words and more describing words

you've lost any grasp on life you had – don't you feel like you've lost all sense of what life is supposed to be?

.

Don't you feel like it's drifted away from you? The point of it all?
And isn't having that thought utterly exhausting and. More than that More than that really Definitely more than that Actually, definitively with the could you just SHUT THE FUCK UP?

.

–   There is a point at which the thought is not enough. The thought can be in my head the thought can exist up here in my head or wherever we carry thoughts perhaps, perhaps it is closer to my heart or my guts or somewhere in my intestines but the thought can

be the thing, the beautiful perfect thing, the thought
can be the Entire World for as long as you are happy
for it to just be the thought and it is like a needle, it
is like a needle has pushed in on my skin and settled
somewhere in my system, big and perfect and whole
but unfinished because you need it to finish you need
it to end and aren't you tired aren't you exhausted
aren't you livid and famished and desperate now
because the thought the thought that seemed simple
is not enough and I think we fucked it up I think we
made a mistake somewhere along the way which is
ludicrous which is desperately desperately desperate
because I think I have been living on the principle of
kindness and hope being enough and the thought being
enough but it turns out it isn't it turns out we stopped
watching and checking and nurturing the thought to
become the action at some point because at some
point I opened my eyes at some point I looked up and
it felt like wastelands and wastelands and wastelands
and wastelands had grown where we thought we were
building mountains because now I stand where I
thought there would be rolling rolling mountains and it
is a little patch of dirt where potatoes and bluebells and
watermelons wouldn't deign to grow let alone progress
let alone a thing like progress because your choice your
choice your choice and my choice have turned out to
be not the fertile soil we thought we were standing two
feet apart upon but dry and arid and empty and alone
because the thought the thought the thought hasn't
been enough hasn't been the thing hasn't been –

Loud noise. It is cold. It is bright. And then it is black.

Act Four

This scene should be between four women.

– I feel ready.

– Are you sure

– I feel completely ready. It feels like an inevitability.

.

– It may take years.

– It probably will.

– Imagine if it took weeks

– Or just one day

– Wouldn't that be fucking

– We're going to dismantle the monetary system

– Yes

– And overthrow the government

– Yes

– We'll expect other countries to follow suit

– Yes

– Quickly, and we have plans in place for that

– Of course

– All jobs will be destroyed

– And all couples broken

– And we take over the airwaves, the televisions, the Internet, etcetera.

.

– And we'll eradicate all men.

.

– Yes.

.

- As a necessity.
- Yes.

.

- You sound sad
- I am sad
- It won't work if you're sad
- It won't work if you aren't.

It failed. The whole world failed at it. It could have been so brilliant. How strange of you not to feel sad.

Who knew that life could be so awful.

.

I CAN HEAR YOU

E.V. CROWE

Characters

DAVID: 60s

RUTH: 40s

ELLIE: 20s

SANDRA: 30s

TOMMY: 20s

All scenes take place in David and Marie's living room.

1.

After the funeral. RUTH brings in trays of sandwiches. DAVID sits on the sofa.

RUTH: It's 41 degrees in Dubai today. I've got an app on my phone that tells you all the temperatures of all the different cities.

DAVID: What does it say about here?

Pause.

RUTH: Fork food.

DAVID: Fork food?

RUTH: It's food you can eat with just a fork.

DAVID: Fork food?

RUTH: Yes.

DAVID: Why's that then?

RUTH: At Mum's, there were a number of people leaning against the wall in the hall trying to juggle everything. There are marks on the wall in the hallway. The hallway's marked.

DAVID: You can eat cake with a fork.

RUTH: Yes.

DAVID: I don't think cake is a bad idea.

RUTH: I'm not just making this up. And looking back, I think that the food at Mum's funeral was misleading. Fork food says funeral. Cake; birthday party.

DAVID: Your Mum would've been happy with a packet of crisps.

RUTH: Yes.

DAVID: Very happy.

RUTH: Well, we've thought it through a bit more this time. And we know what we're doing a bit more. We've been a bit more organised. And it cost a bit more. And we've cleaned the house. And. We know what we're doing this time. Don't we? We're first back, then everyone else comes over in about half an hour.

DAVID: Don't you like cake?

RUTH: No.

Pause.

DAVID: It's been nice having Sandra around.

RUTH: Good.

DAVID: She's on her way.

RUTH: I suspect that really what's playing on Sandra's mind is/

DAVID: She's been terrific.

RUTH: It doesn't actually stop you feeling…I feel responsible for Jim whenever he leaves the house.

DAVID: Do you?

RUTH: Fridays especially. I feel responsible for Jim.

DAVID: He couldn't come then?

RUTH: Who?

DAVID: Jim?

RUTH: Jim can't come. What I mean is, it won't matter what we say because she'll feel responsible for what happened to Tommy. Sandra will blame herself.

SANDRA comes in.

SANDRA: It was open. Sorry.

RUTH: Hello Sandra.

SANDRA waves awkwardly.

SANDRA: Hello Ruth. Hiya David.

SANDRA hovers around DAVID, unsure how to greet him. She bows, awkwardly.

SANDRA: I wanted to say, thanks for that, thanks for going the bit extra on the/

RUTH: No problem.

SANDRA: I know you must have spent a fortune when your mum died too.

RUTH: Honestly, it's/

SANDRA: I said I'll give you a bit towards. I'm going to do that. I've borrowed some from my mum.

RUTH: She's not working at the moment or is she?

SANDRA: She is now, double. I mean. She went from no job to two jobs. She's working two jobs. So she said she'd lend me a bit. It's Dad who's off. She can't come today in fact.

RUTH and SANDRA: She's working.

SANDRA: Exactly.

RUTH: Whenever you can. It doesn't matter really.

SANDRA: I'll get it from her tomorrow. I don't want you lot out of pocket.

RUTH: We won't be. I mean, we would be happy if you want to 'contribute' but it's not essential. In a practical sense. We bought everything we needed. It's all done.

SANDRA looks up upset. DAVID notices.

DAVID: Have you seen all the flowers Sandra? At the church, by the road, in here?

SANDRA: Yes! You have to laugh a bit. Sorry. I just… *(She takes a deep breath.)* You have to laugh a bit. Tommy and flowers! It's a lot.

RUTH: When Mum died, we had a bunch there, a bunch there, and then only one in the hallway. Largely lilies, I got some on my top. It never comes off.

SANDRA: The pollen.

RUTH: You have to 'hoover' it off your top apparently. Don't wipe it. But guess what?

SANDRA: You wiped it.

RUTH: It just smears. So there's a top from Mum's funeral I can't ever wear again.

Pause.

DAVID: Do you think we can stick the match on while we wait?

RUTH: Actually Dad, do you mind if we don't.

Silence.

Is that alright Dad?

DAVID turns it on. The sound of a football game on. DAVID watches the TV.

DAVID: Tommy would want to know the score.

RUTH: Well.

DAVID: At least to know the score.

SANDRA: Tommy was exactly the same!

RUTH: *(To SANDRA.)* Let me get you a drink.

DAVID: I'll have a beer, love.

RUTH goes.

SANDRA: Tommy really liked watching…TV.

DAVID: He was my only son.

SANDRA and DAVID sit in silence.

RUTH comes back with a beer for DAVID.

RUTH: We should do a toast to Tommy while it's just us.

DAVID's already drinking his beer.

SANDRA: Cheers anyway. I'm not drinking.

RUTH: Are his team all coming round?

SANDRA: Yes.

RUTH: What about work lot?

SANDRA: I expect so. Seems like people have been really affected. I hope none of them are driving home. Do you think we can drive people? I don't mind not drinking. I've had nothing since the accident. Mind if I go and change my tights upstairs. I had to get a spare pair from the garage on the way.

RUTH: OK Sandra.

They go. DAVID sits alone.

RUTH comes back.

RUTH: She looks better.

DAVID: What?

RUTH: She looks a lot better than she did.

DAVID: OK.

RUTH: She's got widow's flush. That's quite a famous thing.

DAVID: What?

RUTH: She's flushed.

DAVID: I can't say I picked up on that.

RUTH: The flush. She doesn't know it but her body knows it.

DAVID: Knows what? They weren't married.

RUTH: No I know.

DAVID: So how can you have widow's flush? I've not heard of it.

RUTH: Yes you have. Someone feels better when they don't have to look after someone anymore. They don't mean to feel like that but they do.

DAVID: Who feels better?

RUTH: What?

DAVID: Who feels better now that Tommy's dead?

RUTH: No one.

DAVID: You just said, someone feels better! Who?

Silence.

RUTH: You'll never guess what she asked me for. A bit of Tommy's hair. A 'lock' of Tommy's hair.

DAVID: What?

RUTH: Mum kept one of us both. It's in her drawer, next to her dresser.

DAVID: Did you give it to her?

RUTH: I said later. She'll forget with any luck.

DAVID: I don't like this kind of talk.

RUTH: Dad!

DAVID: It's girl talk isn't it?

RUTH: We're talking about Sandra.

DAVID: Exactly. Talk to someone else about it. You can talk to someone else.

RUTH: She's depressed. She's been depressed all the time I've known her.

DAVID: What do you mean?

RUTH: Haven't you ever noticed?

DAVID: She's not depressed is she? She's allowed to be depressed today.

RUTH: She's less depressed today.

SANDRA comes down wearing un-laddered tights.

SANDRA: Thanks Ruth. That feels a bit better. I've remembered where it is now. I don't know how I didn't remember it. My head's a bit…all over the place. It's where the Woolworths was. It's just called the 'Crystal shop'. What's funny about it is they're only young. They're not old-fashioned at all. It's sort of a bit trendy. It's a pop-up crystal shop. Do you know those places? Have you seen it? You don't know how long it's open for, they just get to have the old shop for a bit. It's massive anyway. The old Woolworths was big wasn't it. If you think how far back it went where all the kids' toys were. Remember. They're in there. They've made it look nice, rugs and wall hangings. Ellie that's who I met there. She's coming later.

RUTH: What does she call herself, Ellie? What's that word? 'Fortune teller'?!

SANDRA: She just says she's interested and knows a lot about crystals. She said she might be able to help heal up the grieving.

RUTH: Heal it up? She's a 'healer' is she?!

SANDRA: No. She's just. I don't know. I call her Ellie.

Pause.

Do you need help with the putting the food out?
Everything looks very 'Marie'.

RUTH: What do you mean?

SANDRA: It looks how I think if Marie was here, it's how she, well, it's very Marie.

DAVID: We've done it. We got up very early and did it. We did it how Marie would want it.

RUTH: Yes we got up very early and I came down and Dad was literally on his hands and knees scrubbing the floors. Weren't you Dad, just like Mum would've been? And it's Dad's hands that absolutely stink of bleach now.

DAVID observes her sarcasm, SANDRA does not.

And then we had breakfast together by the window and we watched the sun rise. *(Pause.)* It's 40 degrees in Dubai today, Sandra. Imagine that level of sun on your face.

2.

Later that day, after the funeral. DAVID and RUTH, and ELLIE sitting quietly, unnoticed.

RUTH: How many people were there at Mum's do you think?

DAVID: Half.

RUTH: That's what I thought.

DAVID: Tommy's was double.

RUTH: Yes.

DAVID: I was going to ask you.

RUTH: Dad!

DAVID: For a bit? Or not?

RUTH: What?

DAVID: Alright, don't.

RUTH: Hang on a minute.

DAVID: You can be here for a bit can't you.

RUTH: I've got Jim.

DAVID: Oh yes.

RUTH: We did essentially emigrate.

DAVID: Dubai isn't that far though is it?

RUTH: The flights aren't cheap.

DAVID: You haven't been there long.

RUTH: The idea is that we are there, and that's what we're doing.

DAVID: Have you got a job?

RUTH: Not yet.

DAVID: Oh right.

RUTH: Not yet.

DAVID: You should have gone out there sooner then. I thought there were lots of jobs out there.

Pause.

RUTH: We've been thinking about trying. I didn't want to bring it up or anything in case.

DAVID: OK.

RUTH: OK.

DAVID: I don't need to hear about all that then.

RUTH: Um. Well, OK. You just asked so I'm telling you.

DAVID: There are some things, that don't need talking about.

RUTH: I'm just saying that Jim and I, me especially, maybe you don't want to talk it through. You've just said you don't so.

DAVID: I don't know why you two didn't have a kid before.

RUTH: Because I wasn't sure Dad. If that was what I/

DAVID: It's too late now is it?

RUTH: We don't know yet. It probably is. We don't know.

DAVID: How long have you been trying?

RUTH: We haven't yet.

DAVID and RUTH notice ELLIE.

ELLIE: I'm sorry, I'm Sandra. I mean I'm Ellie, I'm waiting for Sandra to bring the car round. She said she wouldn't mind giving me a lift.

RUTH: She's obsessed with other people not driving.

ELLIE: That's right. You're David and you're Ruth! I've heard ever so much/

DAVID: Are you a friend from work?

ELLIE: I work at the old Woolworths.

DAVID: It's you she wanted the 'lock of hair' for?!

ELLIE: That's right. I didn't mean to interrupt. I'm sorry.

RUTH: We didn't see you hiding there.

ELLIE: I wasn't hiding. I was sitting here.

Pause.

DAVID: Is that why you came today? For the hair?

ELLIE: It's more about picking up on things. And Sandra asked me. I think she wanted the moral support.

RUTH: Right.

ELLIE: It was very useful to be able to come. You handled everything, the funeral was, I mean, it was very moving.

DAVID: Do they give you a low rent then? At the old Woolworths?

ELLIE: It's a deal with the Council. It is quite low. But I've always wanted my own shop. I've been looking at the ins and outs of it for years.

DAVID: What did you do before?

RUTH: Dad.

ELLIE: I worked in Woolworths.

DAVID: Oh right! We were all very sad when it closed. Where do you get the crystals from?

ELLIE: What?

DAVID: Where do crystal shops get their crystals from?

ELLIE: Oh. All over. Abroad.

DAVID: Not from Woolworths then?!

ELLIE: *(To RUTH.)* I helped a woman the other day. She was trying for a baby. *(Pause.)* The woman I met. Lovely, really nice lady.

Silence.

We could talk to your mum if you like. I mean we can talk to her. We can try to connect with her. If you wanted to, Ruth.

RUTH: It's OK thanks. I don't think I need to talk to Mum right now.

ELLIE: Sorry I didn't mean to…it's just this woman I met. She wanted to, she thought it would really help. When Sandra told me about your and Tommy's mum dying, the leading up to it and then…I cried. I'd only just met her. I was crying. Such a lovely family. A proper family. It's so unfair.

RUTH: We didn't want to be rude about the crystals, but. It's not really our [thing].

ELLIE: It's OK. I'll talk to Sandra.

RUTH: Yep. Our mum had a nice life, thanks. I wouldn't want to… Leave mum out of this I think. She's dead now so. I don't really want it mixed up in my head with lotions and potions. I'm not really into all that. Thanks. You're a friend of Sandra's. So. Thank you.

ELLIE: That's good.

RUTH: What?

ELLIE: I hope I have a nice life.

RUTH: Yes.

ELLIE: How old was she when she died? If it's OK to ask.

DAVID: 64. 'Devoted mother and wife'.

ELLIE: 64's young isn't it.

RUTH: What does that mean?

ELLIE: Nothing. I don't know. 64.

DAVID: That's what we got engraved on the…inscribed on the…stone. Devoted mother and wife.

ELLIE: Sandra's told me so much about you all.

DAVID: Has she?

ELLIE: I was very happy to be here. To meet you all in person.

DAVID: That's nice.

ELLIE: I ask her about you all the time.

RUTH: Oh.

ELLIE: You're a *family* family.

Pause.

ELLIE: I get interested about people and then I notice
    something and I can't help noticing.

RUTH: What have you noticed?

DAVID: She's here for Sandra.

RUTH: What's she noticed? Am I being stupid?

ELLIE: Nothing.

RUTH: Yes she has. What is it?

Pause.

ELLIE: No it's OK.

RUTH: No go on, I'm interested.

DAVID: Forget it!

RUTH: Yes, forget it, I couldn't care less.

ELLIE looks right at RUTH.

ELLIE: You've got a blockage.

RUTH: Who does?

SANDRA comes in.

SANDRA: Sorry, there was traffic. I'm parked at the front.

SANDRA notices there's a bit of tension.

SANDRA: If it's alright with you two. I'll need that bit of
    Tommy's hair. If it's not a bother. I know we weren't
    officially married. I've got no rights as such to the hair. I
    just feel/

RUTH: I thought you'd want to just go home and rest a bit?

117

SANDRA: Ellie said the energy around Tommy is very high at the moment. So it's easier.

Pause.

The more people thinking about him. The easier it is. The crash was in the news, he's got an obituary in the paper, they've got a memorial at the football house, there's a load of stuff on Facebook. On his Facebook page. Best get it done today. It's about vibrations isn't it? And working out which is the best crystal to unlock things with?

DAVID: Right, OK love. I put it in an envelope by the door.

RUTH: Did you?

DAVID: I gave her the hair. I mean.

He shrugs.

SANDRA: *(To RUTH.)* Thanks love.

RUTH: Alright.

SANDRA: Bye.

ELLIE: OK then.

SANDRA and ELLIE go.

RUTH: What a weirdo.

DAVID: Well.

RUTH: God. Flipping heck. This is Tommy's day.

DAVID: Have they gone?

RUTH: 'Crystal Ellie' was invited yes, but she didn't have to come. She didn't exactly have to come. For 'the energy'. Oh yes! That's right. There's 'a lot of energy around Tommy'. Find your own family. What is she? Orphan Annie?!

'Energy'!?!

What, is she some kind of Shaman? She looks a bit anaemic if you ask me. I don't remember her from the tills at Woolworths that's for sure. It was 'useful' to be here!

DAVID: I remember her.

RUTH: She'd look like a hipster. Definitely too cool for a uniform. God!

Pause.

RUTH: Anyway, we put a lot into today. It was a proper funeral. Well done us. If Tommy was here, he'd be touched. What on earth did she mean. I've got a blockage? A blockage? I have no idea what she's talking about.

SANDRA comes back in.

SANDRA: I just wanted to say sorry about just now. I know I'm a bit. Ellie's so nice. I didn't want her to think I wasn't grateful for trying to help and all of that. It's been really smashing having all the support I've got from you two and. I wanted you to know that I'm not just going to go round the bend. I'm going to do Tommy proud.

DAVID: It's OK Sandra.

SANDRA: No honestly. I applied to do a teaching course.

RUTH: Did you?

SANDRA: I know, seems mad. It does a bit doesn't it? But I think I'll be alright at it, I wasn't sure. But now there's nothing keeping me here and. I'm glad I applied.

RUTH: I thought you said you wanted to stay nearby so you can visit the grave.

SANDRA: I'd be back here and there wouldn't I?

RUTH: It's better than working at the Shell Garage shop.

SANDRA: It is isn't it? I haven't worked there for about two years actually.

RUTH: Oh?

SANDRA: But teaching is better. So anyway. I just didn't want you thinking I'm a weirdo.

RUTH: So where are you working then?

SANDRA: I haven't got in yet, I won't know for a few weeks. But, you know. *(Pause.)* I work at the hotel off the dual carriageway.

RUTH: Sorry, yes you did tell me that. Sorry.

SANDRA: It's lucky your work have given you some family time off.

DAVID: Ruth doesn't work anymore.

SANDRA: Oh.

RUTH: That's not strictly true is it? I'm taking some time, to…

SANDRA: Is it in here?

SANDRA takes the envelope out of her pocket.

SANDRA: Ellie's very excited by, I don't know.

RUTH: Sandra.

SANDRA: We're excited by the possibilities. Of what could be. Without any limitations. That maybe everything is possible.

RUTH: She's probably what 24? She's a 'hipster'.

DAVID: A what?

RUTH: You know. A hipster.

SANDRA sits. Takes out the lock of hair.

SANDRA: I can't help it. It's like strands of gold!

She brushes it to her lips.

SANDRA: Tommy, Tommy, Tommy.

3.

A week later.

RUTH is on the landline telephone.

RUTH: You should make sure you put some factor 30 on…

Well if you do go outside…

Alright…

Yes. Of course we need to be in the same place. Of course! There's no reason why we can't.

I know.

I'll call you later. OK, then. Well maybe we'll speak later.

OK. Yes we'll speak later. I might be busy but OK. Later on. Bye.

DAVID comes in. RUTH hangs up.

RUTH: So how big is it? The notice board?

DAVID: It's big. Was that an international call?

RUTH: He called me. How big? Big as what?

DAVID: It's that whole wall. I didn't hear it ring.

RUTH: You won't be charged for the call. Nothing is going to show up on your bill. Don't worry. *(Pause.)* Next to the bar? What one big photograph?

DAVID: There's a medium-sized picture of him, and then a lot of smaller ones. They wanted me to ask you for a few more.

RUTH: I think they've had the lot.

DAVID: Some kiddy ones.

RUTH: I gave them some ones of him as a kid. You and Tommy at the father and son game.

DAVID: It's like pulling teeth.

RUTH: Not those ones?

DAVID: No, I mean. Yes they'll want them. I just… It's the game coming up so they want a few more. Tommy and I always used to play.

Pause.

RUTH: I could play this year.

Silence.

RUTH: I used to play at school. I'd be a lot faster that half those fatties who run around now.

DAVID looks at her.

RUTH: I'll wear shorts.

DAVID: I don't want to look soppy do I? Asking my daughter to play.

RUTH: What's soppy about that?

DAVID: We used to do the sandwiches that's all.

RUTH: Did you?

DAVID: We did yes.

RUTH: How many did you normally make?

DAVID: A few. We did it every year. Except last year.

RUTH: Egg and cress or tuna mayonnaise?

DAVID: I don't know.

RUTH: So you played and did the sandwiches did you?

DAVID: Well, I played, your mum made the sandwiches.

RUTH: Who did them last year?

DAVID: They were terrible. Substandard.

RUTH: So I can't play, but I can make the sandwiches.

He puts the football game on.

RUTH: Dad.

DAVID looks at her.

SANDRA's coming round.

DAVID looks around in an exaggerated way. He returns to watching the TV.

RUTH: That was the door.

DAVID relents and turns it off.

Did she go upstairs?

SANDRA comes in. She looks distracted.

RUTH: We thought we heard you. I thought you'd gone upstairs.

SANDRA: What? No. I said I'd pop in didn't I?

RUTH: I bumped into your mum. She said you had some news.

SANDRA: Did she? Oh yes. Did she? Yes that's right. I mean I wasn't sure if I was going to say.

I do have a bit of news.

RUTH: Are you OK?

SANDRA: I'm fine. Yes. You're still here?

RUTH: What?

SANDRA: I thought you'd be back at yours and Jim's by now. Back in Dubai.

RUTH: Well I'm not.

SANDRA: What sort of temperature is it now in Dubai? Is it even hotter is it now?

RUTH: Yes it's burn-your-skin-off hot.

TOMMY comes in and sits down.

They look at him.

A moment.

SANDRA: I meant to tell you.

TOMMY: Don't have heart attacks.

SANDRA: Last night.

RUTH: You saw him when he died. You were sitting next to him. Stuck in the car.

SANDRA: Yes.

RUTH: Sandra?

SANDRA: I'm sorry. I didn't realise it would work.

TOMMY: Don't worry I'm just visiting! Have you had your lunch already?

RUTH: Yes.

TOMMY: Any left?

RUTH: Sorry, it went in the bin.

TOMMY: Maybe it's for the best if it's anything like what you put on at the funeral.

RUTH: Didn't you like it? I mean, did you eat it?

TOMMY: I thought it looked terrible.

RUTH: Really?

TOMMY: Bloody disgusting.

DAVID: I hardly ate a thing.

TOMMY: I'm messing with you. I wasn't AT my own funeral. That's weird. Dad isn't the score on?

DAVID: I don't know. I've. We sort of agreed not to have it on anymore when people come round. The girls, they don't like it on in the background.

TOMMY puts it on.

TOMMY: Look, now I can just come here sometimes. Sandra set it up with her mate Ella.

SANDRA: Ellie.

RUTH: How often will you be back?

SANDRA: We haven't sorted it 100% yet because…

TOMMY: Every Sunday. *(To RUTH.)* You can do Mum's roast.

SANDRA: It's just. I got into my course, and…

TOMMY: You never even talked about teaching before.

SANDRA: I applied…

TOMMY: Never, ever mentioned it before. Ever.

RUTH: She didn't that's true.

TOMMY: Come on love. I mean. OK, it's OK. Forget it. I've come back. You asked me to come back and I came. For you.

SANDRA: Is that how it…is that how it works?

TOMMY: I don't even remember the crash. We crashed didn't we? That's right isn't it?

SANDRA: Yep. You were the one…yes.

His eyes flick to the screen. Everyone waits for TOMMY to say something else about it. He doesn't. RUTH touches his arm, full of sympathy, glances at SANDRA.

RUTH: It's good just to get in isn't it, Sandra. It's the getting in bit.

SANDRA: I surprised myself.

RUTH: You don't have to go if what Tommy's saying is…it might change things.

TOMMY: I can do the game with you now on Sunday Dad.

RUTH: I might do it.

TOMMY: It's a father and son game. She can't even run. Have you seen her run?

RUTH: I've been at the gym a bit actually.

SANDRA: I've never seen her run.

RUTH: He can't play football.

DAVID: Sorry son. Ruth's got a point.

RUTH: I was thinking, I could play, and Sandra maybe you could help out and make the sandwiches. By way of a contribution.

SANDRA: Oh. Yes. I know I still owe you a bit don't I. Sorry Ruth. I'm going to get that to you. I'll transfer it online.

RUTH: That's not what I…

SANDRA: Just give me your account details can't you.

RUTH: I don't know if I know them off the top of my head. 30-41-79, then…um…I'll have to look.

SANDRA: I've got an app on my phone if I can find it. It's really easy.

SANDRA rootles around in her bag. TOMMY shakes his head in a superior way.

TOMMY: You lot. You make me laugh.

Pause.

RUTH: Did you see Mum there then?

TOMMY: Um.

RUTH: Did you?

TOMMY: Er, 'see' her?!

RUTH: If you see her…

TOMMY: What?

RUTH: Can you talk to her?

TOMMY: OK I did 'see' her once. She was dancing.

DAVID: Dancing?

TOMMY: Yeah! Dancing. Like this.

TOMMY does a half-dance, his head angled upwards.

RUTH: Tommy what? Mum didn't dance like that, did she?

SANDRA: What are you saying Tommy?

TOMMY: Nothing. She was very quiet.

RUTH: Well which was it, dancing or very quiet?

TOMMY: I think she's…

RUTH: What?

TOMMY reads RUTH's face, provokes.

TOMMY: I think she was a bit upset.

RUTH: What is it?

TOMMY: She was upset you didn't do much for the funeral.

RUTH: 'We'? You were around then Tommy.

TOMMY hold his hands up.

TOMMY: I'm having a laugh! I haven't 'seen' her. Doesn't work like that.

RUTH: Then how does it work?

TOMMY: What? Now everyone wants to hear what I have to say!

RUTH: So she wasn't dancing?

Silence.

RUTH: Ellie's clever. She must be. How did she do it?

SANDRA: She just believes in it. Really really believes in it.

RUTH: Believes in what?

Pause.

TOMMY: A lot of people at mine then were there?

SANDRA: Loads. It was devastating.

TOMMY: How many is loads?

SANDRA: More than there was room for. It got to people.
When someone like you dies young, in their prime of life.

It gets to people, because it feels like a tragedy. It feels like the world has really lost something special. You look at a picture of you Tommy and we think about all that's good and right in the world. People came to look at you dead, and remember what it means to be alive. You make people think of that.

TOMMY: Let's have a look.

He takes a picture of himself off the side.

SANDRA: That's you when you were just finishing school isn't it. All golden looking.

TOMMY: Yes.

TOMMY leans back into the chair, taking the photo of himself with him.

TOMMY: I see what you mean. It is tragic. I see what the word means.

Pause.

TOMMY: Looks like it's just me and you Dad.

DAVID: There's nothing wrong with just me and you!

RUTH: It won't just be you and Dad.

TOMMY: It will. Sandra on her 'course', you in 'Dubai'. Bit weird. Just us. Don't you think. That doesn't make any…I can't picture it.

SANDRA: What do you mean?

TOMMY: I don't know. Just us two?!

SANDRA: Don't say that.

TOMMY: I should go back then.

SANDRA: No!

RUTH: No!

TOMMY: I'm not coming back all the time, just to sit here with Dad.

RUTH: Maybe Sandra doesn't have to be in Birmingham.

SANDRA: It's the course, the way the programme works.

RUTH: You could get the train in. There's a quick one now isn't there.

TOMMY: Why don't you hang around a bit?

RUTH: –

DAVID: She's in Dubai.

RUTH: I'm in Dubai.

TOMMY: I don't even know where that is. Is it even an actual place?

RUTH: Yes it is. It's in the…Emirates.

TOMMY: I thought it was just a visit.

RUTH: No, the plan was always to stay.

TOMMY: Why?

RUTH: We've made our life there. We have a new life there. With everything just how we want it.

TOMMY: What did you want to talk to Mum for?

RUTH: I don't. Nothing.

TOMMY: What did you want me to ask her?

RUTH: Nothing.

SANDRA: Maybe it is possible to speak to her.

RUTH: There isn't anything except maybe hello or…hello.

TOMMY: Yes there was.

DAVID: Her and Jim are trying.

TOMMY: Trying what?

SANDRA: Trying for a baby?

TOMMY: So what do you want to talk to Mum about?

RUTH: I don't.

TOMMY: What do you want to know?

RUTH: Nothing!

TOMMY: I can tell. Just say, what do you want to talk to her about. What do you want to know then?

Pause.

RUTH: If it was worthwhile.

TOMMY: If what was?

RUTH: All of it. Being a mother.

4.

A few days later. RUTH, DAVID, SANDRA and ELLIE are gathered.

ELLIE: If you could just like move your chairs round a bit, so it's a bit more of a…like a semi-circle. And then what I tried to do last time with Sandra, was to keep the energy quite strong but still and…OK?

So Sandra…you had something you wanted to ask.

SANDRA: I wanted to know. If we'll be able to tell the difference. I mean, if Marie hears us but doesn't want to come, will that feel different to…if the process just doesn't work and we don't hear anything?

ELLIE doesn't answer. She takes a crystal out of her bag, hands it to RUTH.

ELLIE: Blue Lace Agate. It's been used for thousands of years by different civilisations, to help people locate their inner voice and to calm their fears. It helps to unblock miscommunications and in a world of noise to help the holder say what's on their mind.

SANDRA: I thought we were using the pendulum.

ELLIE: We are, this is just for Ruth.

RUTH: Um. OK.

RUTH takes it, drops it in her lap.

RUTH: Thanks.

ELLIE: Let's just try shall we?

RUTH: Let's.

SANDRA: We're doing this for Marie.

DAVID: That's right Sandra.

ELLIE: We have to be sure that we're asking your mum to come back for her own sake, for who she is in the universe.

DAVID: Don't ask her anything too much.

RUTH: We've agreed we won't.

Pause.

RUTH: We want Mum back, just, because. Because we love
her. She's our mum. And we're all here, it's like it was.
She's a part of that.

SANDRA opens her hand.

RUTH: What's this one?

ELLIE: Copal.

ELLIE lifts the crystal on a piece of string so it hangs in the air.

RUTH: Copal?

ELLIE: When Tommy came back, we did the same. We asked
the universe to help us. We channelled a strong energy
flow through the copal to Tommy and asked him. Do you
want to speak with us, yes or no?

If the copal swung to the left it meant yes. If it swung to the
right it meant no.

It swung to the left…and then he came home.

Please, the items you've brought with you.

*RUTH takes out a small leather notebook, puts it on the floor in front
of ELLIE. DAVID puts down a ring. SANDRA puts down a postcard.*

SANDRA: This is all I…

SANDRA then also puts down a pearl necklace.

RUTH: Is that Mum's necklace?

SANDRA: Yes.

RUTH: Where did you get that from?

SANDRA: Tommy gave it to me.

RUTH: Dad is this true?

DAVID: No idea.

SANDRA: I promise. Of course. I assumed she gave it to
Tommy.

RUTH: Well that's just…well.

ELLIE: Let's just try and use it shall we. For the purpose of today. If we get hold of her, you can ask her yourselves?

RUTH: Hmm.

SANDRA: She did.

RUTH: Yup.

SANDRA: This is a postcard Tommy and I wrote to her that we forgot to send, from when we were in Spain. I wrote the address and everything but then we never passed a place that sold stamps. And then I meant to give it to her but I never did. So.

Pause.

We had a good time on that one.

RUTH: These are Mum's recipes. Christmas cake etc. Nice stuff.

SANDRA: Has it got that casserole in it?

RUTH: Yup.

SANDRA: I'd like to get that. The nice lamb one?

RUTH: Yes.

ELLIE: I asked one of you to bring a photograph or a letter.

DAVID: I chucked all the letters. This is her wedding ring. But she stopped wearing it after…she put on weight.

ELLIE: OK so.

SANDRA: What happens now?

ELLIE: I was just about to say. Ruth, do you have your crystal? It will help you to communicate your feelings.

RUTH: Oh, I can't find it.

RUTH looks half-heartedly under her legs.

RUTH: I'll find it later. I will communicate as best I can without it…!

ELLIE: You don't believe it can help?

RUTH: Um…

RUTH laughs it off.

ELLIE: OK. So what I need everyone to do is to close your eyes, and think of a memory of your mother. What was her name? Marie?

DAVID: 'Mum'.

ELLIE: Mum?

DAVID: We all…yes. Mum.

Pause.

ELLIE: Think of your mother, mother-in-law, wife, 'Mum'.

Everyone closes their eyes. ELLIE gathers up the things. She puts a small bowl of crystals, from her handbag on top. She holds up the pendulum.

ELLIE: 'Mum', do you wish to speak to us?

RUTH: We're just asking that?

ELLIE: What do you want to ask her?

RUTH: Does she want to come back?

ELLIE: I think it's the same thing isn't it?

RUTH: Is it?

ELLIE: Let's just… Let's see.

The pendulum doesn't move.

ELLIE: Marie we want to speak to you, do you wish to reply?

Silence.

RUTH: I don't think it's going to work.

ELLIE: Please just one…

RUTH: I don't think it's going to work.

ELLIE: It might work.

RUTH: It won't.

ELLIE: We don't know for a fact that it won't work.

RUTH: These things don't.

SANDRA: Tommy came back.

RUTH: That's…yes…he did.

ELLIE: I try to stay positive. It's only early on.

They close their eyes.

ELLIE: Marie/

RUTH: Look, Ellie, we brought all the things you asked didn't
   we. I don't understand why it isn't working.

SANDRA: If it doesn't work, we can try again another time.

RUTH: That might take ages.

SANDRA: What's the rush?

RUTH: No nothing. There is no real rush I suppose.

ELLIE: Um. I know that you've all tried really hard but, I did
   actually sort of specifically say that I wanted you to bring
   things that showed the universe that you believed that your
   mum mattered and was 'of importance' on a bigger than
   just herself scale. That she mattered sort of generally. That
   was the…I was under that impression.

   You've brought a recipe book that she used to cook for you
   with, a ring she doesn't wear, a necklace you maybe sort of
   stole, and a postcard from your holiday you couldn't be…
   you didn't send. I'm not being funny. But when Sandra
   wanted Tommy back – there was hair, clothing, awards,
   photos, newspaper clippings.

SANDRA: But Tommy was, a more in the world person.

RUTH looks at her.

SANDRA: In a way.

RUTH: Let's try one more time.

ELLIE shuts her eyes, they all do. She holds up the pendulum.

ELLIE: Marie, do you wish to come back to us?

*The pendulum swings very clearly to the right; 'no'. ELLIE looks
up, no one else has seen, except DAVID. ELLIE and DAVID look at
each other.*

The others open their eyes.

RUTH: Nothing?

ELLIE picks up her things gently.

ELLIE: Look, the pop-up opens in an hour. I can come again tomorrow if you like, we can try again. *(Pause.)* I'll have to check when we open.

RUTH: OK well we'll see.

SANDRA: OK thanks Ellie, thanks so much, thank you for trying Ellie. I love your dress by the way.

ELLIE: Oh.

SANDRA: Really.

ELLIE: It's nothing, it's a bit vintage that's all.

SANDRA: There are a lot of vintage shops now in Birmingham. I like old things.

ELLIE: Yes.

Pause.

RUTH: Thanks Ellie. OK thanks now.

ELLIE: I am sorry Ruth.

RUTH: I don't know why she's saying sorry to me in particular.

ELLIE goes.

RUTH: It was for all of us. I don't know why she's fussing over me.

Silence.

TOMMY comes in.

TOMMY: Budge up.

He puts the TV on.

Sound of the football game. TOMMY leans forward.

RUTH: Sandra/

TOMMY cuts her off, squirming for room in the sofa.

TOMMY: How was the father and son game without a son in the end? I've not heard a peep.

Pause.

DAVID: She got sent off.

TOMMY: What for?

RUTH: I was playing too aggressively. It was considered 'ungentlemanly'.

TOMMY: For fucksake!

RUTH: I couldn't help it. I wanted to punch someone in the face. I did. I was ungentlemanly…

Mum would do anything for us. *(Pause.)* Dad do you think Mum didn't want to speak to us? Do you think she feels let down by us? Is she annoyed at us? Didn't she have a nice life? Wasn't she happy here? Why doesn't she want to talk to us? What have we done wrong? Does she think I should stay and…? Does she think I'm selfish? Why doesn't she want to come back? We can't assume that she even heard us. Do you think she heard us? What does it mean if she doesn't want to come back?

DAVID gets up and puts his hands in his pockets, walks around the room a little.

DAVID: *(As if wrapping things up.)* We won't know. Maybe she didn't hear us.

RUTH: It means something doesn't it. I just don't know what.

Pause.

TOMMY: Seriously, can you move all this crap off the floor please I've got nowhere to put my feet. Have you talked to Jim yet Ruth, have you told him you're staying?

RUTH slides off the sofa onto her knees on the floor and gathers the book, the postcard, the necklace and the ring to her chest with one arm.

The phone rings. DAVID picks up.

DAVID: Yes?

He looks at RUTH, covers the mouthpiece with his hand.

RUTH: The little blue crystal…

DAVID: Ruth, it's Jim again. Here you are, speak to him.

She searches the floor with her hand, patting it repeatedly.

RUTH: Hang on. I can't find it.

END

THIS IS NOT AN EXIT

ABI ZAKARIAN

I would like to thank everyone at the RSC, including the following amazing women:

Pippa Hill, Erica Whyman, Réjane Collard and Collette McCarthy, for all their support and time. Thanks to Julie LeGrand, Ruth Gemmell, Mimi Ndweni and Scarlett Brookes for all their talent, strength and fearlessness. Huge thanks to Jo McInnes for her incredible vision and, especially massive thanks to Sarah Dickenson, for her unbelievable creativity and generosity.

Characters

NORA	WOMAN
BLANCHE	WOMAN
GULCH	WOMAN
RIPLEY	WOMAN

SCENE ONE: THIS IS NOT A MEMORY

NORA and her laptop.
She is trying to write.
The cursor flashes.

After a while:

NORA
There must be a memory before all this. Before I knew who or what I was.

We went on a picnic. Mum packed a wicker basket with sandwiches; ham and cheese, and a bottle of squash. There were chocolate biscuits and apples. Dad carried the basket and a gingham tablecloth to the picnic site. We were on a hill overlooking rolling fields. The sun was shining and it was hot and dry. They both smiled all the time and after we played with a frisbee and then I made a daisy chain and wore it on my head. Dad packed up the picnic whilst Mum shook out the crumbs from the tablecloth. And then we went back downhill and drove home.

I must have a memory before all this.

She puts the laptop down, looks at the screen, reads:

21 Reasons Why Mother Knows Best

BLACKOUT.

SCENE TWO: 21 REASONS WHY MOTHER KNOWS BEST

It's night. NORA is huddled by the radiator. She has a floral pillowcase over her head.

The laptop is whirring and staring at her. There's a pile of magazines beside it.

At the other end of the radiator is BLANCHE.

BLANCHE
There's a smell coming from beneath the fridge.

NORA
I know.

BLANCHE
I had to sniff it out at first. There's some kind of residue in the narrow bit by the sink. You'll probably need to pull the whole thing out to get to it.

NORA
I think it's a mouse.

BLANCHE
Only a mouse? Not biting back now is it?

Beat.

Where do you put the recycling? I couldn't see.

NORA
I've not kept up with it.

BLANCHE
Well you should. It's important. They send you the info and the boxes. You don't actually have to do anything.

NORA
I know.

BLANCHE
You've been in this excuse for a flat for seven years. Rattling around like a dried pea.

NORA
I know.

BLANCHE
We've all got to do our bit.

NORA
I. Know.

BLANCHE scrutinizes the pillowcase.

BLANCHE
Is that Laura Ashley?

NORA
Cath Kidston actually.

BLANCHE
I never liked florals. Your father did the chintz. Reminded him of Granny, along with spotted dick.

Beat.

So how's it going in there?

Pause.

BLANCHE
Oddly this reminds me of that protest I went on when I
was eight months pregnant with you. I'd waddled my way
across Hyde Park with the other women and we handcuffed
ourselves to the railings outside the ministry of work and
pensions. God was I relieved to sit down. But you didn't want
to settle. You wriggled with such excitement that by the time
they brought the wire cutters there was quite a puddle on the
pavement. I like to think it was your first political gesture,
peeing all over the patriarchy. Even the bobby offered me his
hanky.

So…

You ready to agitate?
Spit.
Scratch.
Scream.
THE TIME IS NOW!

NORA is silent.

Didn't think so.

*BLANCHE is bored. She fishes about in NORA's magazine pile and picks
one out.*

879 Jeans That Make You Look Thinner.

NORA
What do you want Mum?

BLANCHE
Who reads this rubbish?

'Why it's time to listen to your inner lioness…'

NORA
Oh God.

BLANCHE reads the screen of NORA's laptop.

21 Reasons Why Mother Knows Best.

ABI ZAKARIAN

BLANCHE
Do you quote me?

NORA
No.

BLANCHE
You know, I might be able to bump it up a bit. Get you a few extra bob.

NORA
This isn't helping.

BLANCHE
Number 1: She always gives the nicest hugs…
Number 2: She'll tell you like it is….

NORA
Straightforward and honest.

BLANCHE
3. Eat with your mouth closed.

NORA
You have to spell it out for them.

BLANCHE
4. Her glass is always half full.
5. Her stitch in time saves nine.
6. She'll make do and mend!/

NORA
Looking back to look forward. It's supposed to respond to the spirit of austerity.

BLANCHE
7. She'll always have tea on the table.
8. Only her recipes work.

NORA
I'm working it up Mum.

BLANCHE
Number 17. She's honest about your weight.

NORA
Obesity crisis.

BLANCHE
18. She knows slimming tricks for bulging bits.
19. She can take it in AND take it out.

NORA
OK you've made your point.

BLANCHE
20. Her love is unconditional.

NORA
Will you please/

BLANCHE
21. Her experience really counts.

NORA (Lifting the pillowcase up.)
SHUT THE FUCK UP!

Pause.

BLANCHE
You know, on second thoughts, I don't think I do have anything to add. You seem to have it all covered.

Long pause.

BLANCHE
What must you think of me?

NORA
Please don't overreact.

BLANCHE
OK.

NORA
It's only a magazine, Mum.

BLANCHE
I was prepared for you to be many things, darling, but naïve wasn't one of them.

NORA
It's light, it's a bit of fun!

BLANCHE
And as you always tell me, I know nothing about that.

She takes back the computer and types with one finger.

Number 22: Because she fought for equal pay.

NORA
Well...you didn't succeed.

BLANCHE
We got it into law.

NORA
Which still isn't working.

BLANCHE
Then keep fighting!

Beat.

NORA
Look I don't want the argument. It's alienating. It's aggressive
It doesn't sell magazines. It doesn't help.

BLANCHE
I should go.

NORA
No.

BLANCHE
You want me to stay?

NORA
No.

BLANCHE
What do you want Nora?

NORA
If I told you would you listen?

BLANCHE
If there's actually something to hear.

NORA has nothing.

NORA
Mum...

BLANCHE gets up to go.

BLANCHE
Sweetie, I am so proud of you. Just look at everything you've

done. You must be so pleased. What a wonderful little woman you are.

BLANCHE has gone.

NORA replaces the pillowcase.

BLACKOUT.

SCENE 3: FINDING YOUR INNER LIONESS

The heart of the night. Pitch black at the window.

NORA is huddled on the sofa with pillowcase back over her head clutching her laptop like a comfort blanket.

Also in the room is GULCH.

GULCH clears her throat.

GULCH
We're going to find your inner lioness.

NORA
My what?

GULCH
Now, I thought we'd begin with a little exercise I call the Super Urgent slash Important Matrix.

NORA
Can we do a different one?

GULCH
So… We've got a lot of ground to cover in this session so are you happy if I manage the time?

NORA
I'm not sure.

GULCH
Is negativity your friend? Because we have to leave that at the door.

Give me three things you would change about yourself if money was not an option.

NORA just looks at her.

Come on, quickly! Three!

NORA tries.

I have to admit you're surprising me here, Nora. I'd expect you to be a pro at this by now. All those enticing cover lines...

You had a vision when you were sucking up to the editorial committee.

NORA
Sorry?

GULCH
I was impressed.

Listen to me. I broke so many heels trampling over the bodies; Everyone so *sensitive*...nearly broke me it did; all that *banter*. Lying there on the boardroom floor with all that broken glass in tiny little pieces, surrounding you. But I navigated that minefield. Man up. Or what's the other option? I have a 99 percent hit rate with my clients. That is fucking amazing isn't it? But you know what? That one percent...she just couldn't cut it. I tried so hard but the fact remains she opened the window, she stepped out of it and *she* ruined a perfectly lovely zen garden 29 floors below.

GULCH removes NORA's pillowcase.

Carrot stick?

NORA
No thanks.

GULCH
They're organic.

NORA
No. I have an allergy.

GULCH gets out her phone, setting the camera and holding it up to take a pic of them.

What are you doing?

GULCH
We're mapping our now.

NORA
Mapping our what?

GULCH
Our now. Seize it. When you can see it you can seize it. Smile.

She takes the picture of them.

GULCH *(Still with the phone, swiping through to pics.)*
Here. Visual stimulus is always good.

NORA looks through the pictures.

GULCH
That's Clara. 7 months. Perfection.

NORA
You have a child?

GULCH
You want one? You get one!

Look at me Nora, look at me. You are worth more.

GULCH goes across to her bag and puts it on the table. She pats it like a puppy.

Valextra. That's twelve hundred pounds of worth right there.

NORA
It's beautiful.

GULCH
Last year's bonus.

She points to the picture of CLARA.

This year's bonus.

And I am not thirty until August.

You can have it all.

But while you're wasting your time moping about someone else is making your money, meeting your husband and living your life. You're not in your twenties anymore. Hell, you're not even in your thirties. The time is now!

Dream it! Live it! Be it!

BELIEVE

In you. In your choices. In your vision. You. Be the CEO of You Enterprises.

We're going to find your inner lioness.

GULCH is very convincing.

GULCH
Come with me Nora. Stay with me. It's a jungle out there.
Lions! Tigers! Bears! Carnivores up every tree.

GULCH demonstrates lion claws.

Grrr.

NORA
Really?

GULCH
Really.

GULCH takes the laptop off NORA and puts it down elsewhere. She then pushes her on all fours and then gets down next to her.

GULCH *(Cont.)*
Grrr.

NORA
Grr?

GULCH
Really attack it. Go for it. Lioness!

NORA
Grrr!

GULCH
Do the claws!

She mimes the claws to NORA.

NORA *(Doing the lion claws.)*
Grrr!

They do the lion claws and growl at each other, circling.

GULCH.
Can you see it Nora? Can you see it? There it is Nora! There
it is
Your 2.4,
Your silver fox,
Your labrador,
Your Tuscan Villa holiday,

NORA
Handbags, softer skin, fiscal freedom/

GULCH
Your Coco de Mer lovebeads,
Your 600 count Egyptian cotton bedsheets, your delightful
family get togethers in yurts on a beach in Norfolk.

NORA roars.

*RIPLEY appears dancing. She's fabulous. Twenty times more fabulous
than you can imagine.*

She raps.

She sees NORA with a WTF look on her face and rushes towards her.

RIPLEY
RRRRRR GEEEE! It's YOU.
I've followed you on Twitter, I've googled you. I've read
everything you write.
You have changed my life.
Number 86, Dojo, 7ForAllMankind.
Half price in TK MAXX. RESULT: ARSE TO DIE FOR.

NORA
Actually that's not one of mine.

RIPLEY
Ah…ok!

NORA
I didn't write that one.

RIPLEY
Yes you did.

NORA
What are you doing here?

RIPLEY
I'm dancing.

NORA
I can see that, but why here?

RIPLEY
Because you like it?

NORA
Do I?

RIPLEY
Yes you do.

She does a little twerk.

Ho, you look like shit.

NORA
What?

RIPLEY
Did you do a no make-up selfie?

NORA
No.

RIPLEY
Good call. Not always good to shatter that illusion. Even for cancer.

NORA
What?

RIPLEY
Just saying.

NORA
You're disgusting.

RIPLEY
Alright.

RIPLEY wanders around the room and goes to sit.

NORA
Don't sit in that.

RIPLEY
So what you doing?

NORA
We're workshopping.

RIPLEY
Workshopping what?

NORA
My inner lioness, actually.

RIPLEY
That's cool.
I can relate.
That's earthy.

Proceed.

Please.

Go.

NORA roars.
RIPLEY roars back.
NORA roars.
They look at GULCH.

GULCH
Keep roaring.

NORA roars again.

GULCH
Now move through the jungle.

NORA
I'm moving!

GULCH
Growl at the tiny creatures in your path.

NORA
I am fucking growling.

GULCH
They're scampering away, look!

NORA
I can see them.

GULCH
You're at the edge of the jungle now.

NORA
Yes, yes, I can see it.

GULCH
That's your future.

NORA
I know, I know.

GULCH

Your future is coming closer and closer, Nora. You're prowling magnificently towards it.

NORA

I'm there. I'm almost there.

GULCH

Channel it now, Nora, channel it! See it. Step out from the jungle, into the bright light and see it…

Can you see it Nora? There it is! There it is Nora! Can you see it?

NORA

NO, I can't!
I AM EXHAUSTED!
40 years of this shit!

BLACKOUT.

SCENE FOUR: THIS IS NOT AN EXIT

The room as before. It is still night.
NORA is near passed out.
The pillowcase is back on her head.
GULCH lays motionless on the floor like a powered-down robot.

RIPLEY is by NORA looking over her shoulder at the laptop.

RIPLEY

I'm a wall, and there's all these people throwing stuff at me. I have to just stand there, back up against the wall with crap on my arms, shit in my hair and a smile on my face while they dig their stubby fingernails in the ground and grab and sling.

And before I know it it's like I'm navigating a minefield. Picking my way through all their random shit. Who the fuck laid those mines? They need to get the UN or something to clear it up; I can't be doing with a minefield; I've got places to be. But I'm not lying down, I'm not hiding, I'm not giving in. I get their patterns, I learn their tricks, I make my choices, for me. Then I get fluid, I adapt.

NORA

What do you know, you're just a girl?

RIPLEY
Ain't you heard lady, there ain't no girls anymore?
Chill out, yeah, you're not all that.

GULCH suddenly sits up.

GULCH
Don't worry, I'm early.

NORA
Oh.

GULCH looks expectant.

Just give me one sec.

NORA suddenly jumps and goes to the back of the room and puts the pillowcase on like a scarf around her shoulders.

GULCH starts to scroll through NORA's laptop.

GULCH
How long have you been here now?

NORA
7… Months.

I'm sorry, everywhere's such a mess.

NORA dashes back and grabs the laptop from GULCH.

Just working it up.

RIPLEY
Let me make your hair all nice.

RIPLEY touches NORA's hair.

NORA
No, I'd rather you didn't.

RIPLEY
Come on. Fix up, look smart.

NORA
No don't.

GULCH
I have the number of a miraculous interior designer. I'll vcard you the details.

RIPLEY starts fiddling with NORA's hair.

NORA
I said – DON'T.

RIPLEY
Jesus, you need to calm down.

NORA
I would if you'd stop sticking your tits in my face.

RIPLEY
Why? What's wrong with them?

NORA
Nothing. Nothing's wrong with them.

RIPLEY
Then what is your issue?

NORA
They're not your only assets.

RIPLEY
Tweet me. *(Meaning fuck off.)*

GULCH
Oh, lovely. Givenchy?

RIPLEY
McQueen.

GULCH
This season?

RIPLEY
eBay.

GULCH
Ouch.

RIPLEY
I thought she farted unicorns.

NORA
So

GULCH
So

NORA
So

GULCH sniffs as though there's a terrible smell.

NORA
Sorry can I get you something?

GULCH
Actually I'm on the 5.2.

NORA
But you don't need/

GULCH
No, I know… But you know.

NORA
I do.

RIPLEY
Three more days on the pepper diet then I can hit up my blog with a new set of belfies.

RIPLEY sits down next to GULCH. They are opposite NORA. It looks like an interview.

RIPLEY
Listen Lady, don't you look down your nose at me.

GULCH sniffs again.

You've been sniffing at me since I came in.

GULCH keeps sniffing.

RIPLEY
Looking me up and down. Judging me.

NORA
No I haven't.

RIPLEY
You stinking of that rank Lady Millionaire shit.

GULCH
That, my little slut, is the sweet smell of success.

RIPLEY
At least I'm not frigid! Helmet hair.

RIPLEY squares up to NORA.

GULCH *(To RIPLEY.)*
Do we know one another?

RIPLEY
Dunno.

GULCH
I read Little Grey Rabbit to deprived slash at-risk toddlers.
Are you one of the mums?

RIPLEY
Nah, it weren't me.

GULCH *(Turning back to NORA.)*
So…

NORA
So

RIPLEY
SO.

NORA
I'm a bit behind deadline.

GULCH
Had a little panic?

RIPLEY
Well we're here now.

Won't take much to stop retweeting your top tips.

Beat.

NORA
You just don't give a fuck do you?

RIPLEY
Oh, I give a fuck.

NORA
Can we reschedule?

RIPLEY
I just don't give a fuck about you.

NORA
What does your week look like?

GULCH
Sixty hours plus.

RIPLEY
How *old* are you?

GULCH
Sixty plus.

NORA
It's intense.

RIPLEY
Over 50?

GULCH
It's stimulating.

RIPLEY
Under 45?

NORA
And then what?

GULCH
Work, work, work.

NORA
Twerk. Twerk. Twerk.

RIPLEY
Don't be naïve Nora.

NORA
It's how the economy is run.

GULCH
Get it while it's good.

RIPLEY
I got snapchatted 31 dick pics today.

NORA
At least I'm not frigid, helmet hair.

Beat.

RIPLEY
What box are you?

NORA
WHAT?

GULCH
You have to stay in the game or the game will keep playing without you.

NORA
What?

GULCH
Your box, Lady.

NORA
What?

RIPLEY
What tick?

NORA
Are you happy?

GULCH
35 to 44? 45 to 54? 55 and older?

NORA
Are you happy?

RIPLEY
What tick?

NORA
Are you happy?

GULCH
Tick Tock Tick Tock Tick Tock/ Tick Tock Tick Tock Tick Tock.

RIPLEY/NORA/GULCH
You are so scared.

GULCH
I'm updating my blog next week. I've got three more days on the pepper diet and I'll be looking fine.

RIPLEY
Check it out, learn something.

NORA
I love your hair like that.

GULCH
It's way too late for you. Bitch.

RIPLEY
Retweet.

GULCH
Fucking hell…yeah.

RIPLEY
Retweet.

GULCH
At least I'm not frigid.

RIPLEY
Retweet.

NORA
You can't have it all, where would you put it?

NORA jumps up and grabs her laptop, she scuttles under the table and starts typing frantically.

RIPLEY
I could have sworn you were one of the mums.

GULCH
Valextra.

RIPLEY
Thirty thousand pounds of worth.

GULCH
Thirty Thousand dick pics.

RIPLEY
Look, you don't know me Lady.

GULCH
Are you taking the piss?

NORA tries to roar under the table as she types. What she types appears projected behind her:

You can't have it all, where would you put it?

*this is typed by NORA again and again so the screen slowly fills. The line is the same but in different layouts.

GULCH
What was that?

NORA squawks and continues typing.

RIPLEY
Oh ease up Shakespeare.

NORA squeaks like a mouse.

RIPLEY
We're mapping our NOW.

She does a little twerk. NORA squeaks.

GULCH
You are fit. End of.

GULCH does a substantial twerk. NORA squeaks and starts to scamper.

RIPLEY
Do the claws.

NORA squeaks.

RIPLEY and GULCH both get down on the floor and start sniffing about for what's squeaking.

Both RIPLEY and GULCH *(Sing song.)*
Come out, come out, Lady Millionaire!

NORA stops typing and becomes aware of the lions about her.
RIPLEY and GULCH start growling.
They prowl around her. She scampers out.
There's chaos.

NORA stands bolt upright and bursts into a note like an opera singer.

BLACKOUT.

SCENE FIVE: THE TIME IS NOW

Dawn is breaking outside. The room is littered with the debris. Against the radiator is BLANCHE, staring at NORA. The pillowcase is gone, as are RIPLEY and GULCH.

BLANCHE
I could never stop you from singing. You'd sing everywhere we went. In the trolley at the supermarket, all the way home in

the back of the car. You had a terrible voice, your sound was 'unique', but you didn't care, you just kept at it. Full-throated bellowing. I could always hear you coming home. I'd think, there she is, my Nora, deafening us all with her caterwauling, marching down the street with her arms outstretched, ready for the world to hear.

And then you lost your tune and didn't look for another.

NORA
No one wanted to listen.

BLANCHE
Yes they did.

Pause.

NORA
The situation's desperate.

BLANCHE
You're right.

NORA
I think it's my fault.

BLANCHE smiles.

NORA
Where do I start?

BLANCHE
Anywhere you wish.

Pause. NORA turns away from BLANCHE, moves back to the computer screen and looks again at what she's written. She scrolls up and down and considers it for one last moment.

Then she hits the touchpad.

Delete?

Pause.

Yes.

Pause.

Select all.

The tiniest hesitation but…

Delete.

And finally, after a little while, it comes…

I do have a memory of before all this. It was winter and I was wrapped up warm in a bright red snow suit and bright blue wellies (which I loved) and you held my hand as we ran, breathless, through fallen leaves and jumped in puddles and counted the crows on the power lines. And there was a woman who you knew, but didn't, but knew a bit, who came floating towards us all shopping and floral headscarf and knee-length boots crying what a lovely son you had, what a lovely boy. And I saw clearly the beautiful, slim, tan leather of her boots next to the mucky, fading rubber of my own. But you didn't correct her. And so neither did I. You just winked at me as we watched her mac belt swing behind her like a tail and then ran indoors to miss the rain and eat club biscuits and make goblets out of their wrappers for my toys to use. And we sang and giggled and danced and played and talked and dreamed and pretended to be small acorns growing into great oaks in the middle of the living room floor. Touch the sky, Nora, you said, touch the sky.

Keep reaching.

The sun rises fully, flooding the room full of morning light.

A dawn chorus of voices singing together in tune.

BLACKOUT.

WWW.OBERONBOOKS.COM

 Follow us on www.twitter.com/@oberonbooks
& www.facebook.com/oberonbook